What peopl

Albion's S

Guy Mankowski has written the book I've been wanting to read for years.

Albion's Secret History is a highly intelligent and loving meditation on creativity and artistic freedoms, pursued over decades by a host of innovators, to those who had previously been denied on the basis of their position within English culture. Mankowski joins so many beautiful dots and creates a mesmerising story of social struggle and the shock and influence of the new. Magnificent and truly brilliant.
Daniel Gothard, author of *Reunited* and *Simon Says*

No future in England's Dreaming? The gleaming fragments of the nation's cultural and countercultural histories unearthed by Guy Mankowski's *Albion's Secret History* suggest otherwise.
Karl Whitney, author of *Hit Factories: A Journey Through the Industrial Cities of British Pop*

Already recognised as a major rising talent, Mankowski here establishes himself as a significant voice.
Andrew Crumey, Man Booker longlisted author of *Sputnik Caledonia*

The most illuminating odyssey through lost, hidden or forgotten English pop culture since Michael Bracewell's *England Is Mine*.
Rhian E. Jones, author of *Clampdown: Pop-Cultural Wars on Class and Gender*

This is a superbly written book, where Mankowski tells how uncomfortable, awkward and magnificent it is to be English. It tells of a scary and beautiful world of musical geniuses, mavericks, chameleons, perverts and wizards, who thought that England was theirs and that it owed them a living, turning Albion into a treasure that everybody with a decent taste in music and some sense of humour can cherish.

Giacomo Bottà, Adjunct Professor in Urban Studies and Music Research, University of Helsinki

Albion's Secret History is a searing discussion of England. Through his snapshots of cultural history, Mankowski explores the form and shape of English identity to reveal who we are, who we've been, and who we'd like to be.

Dr Jon Coburn, Lecturer in History and Heritage, University of Lincoln

Albion's Secret History

Snapshots of England's Pop Rebels and Outsiders

Albion's Secret History

Snapshots of England's Pop Rebels and Outsiders

Guy Mankowski

Winchester, UK
Washington, USA

JOHN HUNT PUBLISHING

First published by Zero Books, 2021
Zero Books is an imprint of John Hunt Publishing Ltd., No. 3 East St., Alresford,
Hampshire SO24 9EE, UK
office@jhpbooks.com
www.johnhuntpublishing.com
www.zero-books.net

For distributor details and how to order please visit the 'Ordering' section on our website.

Text copyright: Guy Mankowski 2020
Cover photograph: Lizzie Jackson

ISBN: 978 1 78904 028 9
978 1 78904 029 6 (ebook)
Library of Congress Control Number: 2020934445

A CIP catalogue record for this book is available from the British Library.

Design: Stuart Davies

UK: Printed and bound by CPI Group (UK) Ltd, Croydon, CR0 4YY

We operate a distinctive and ethical publishing philosophy in
all areas of our business, from our global network of authors to
production and worldwide distribution.

Contents

Also by Guy Mankowski

The Intimates (Legend Press, 2011) ISBN-10: 1907756469
Letters from Yelena (Legend Press, 2012) ISBN-10: 1909039101
How I Left the National Grid (Roundfire, 2014)
ISBN-10: 178279896X
An Honest Deceit (Urbane Publications, 2015)
ISBN-10: 191112997X

This book is dedicated to Stanley Firmin. An example of a fine Englishman.

Preface

This volume compiles snapshots of English pop culture's rebels and outsiders – from Evelyn Waugh to PJ Harvey via The Long Blondes and The Libertines. By focusing on cultural figures who served to define England, this book looks at those who have *really* shaped Albion's secret history – not just its oft-quoted official cultural history, so frequently recited for Olympic Ceremonies and other self-congratulatory retrospectives and impotent shows of capital.

By departing from the narrative that dutifully follows The Beatles, The Rolling Stones, The Sex Pistols and Oasis and by instead penetrating the surface of England's pop history (including the venues it was shaped in) this piece throws new light on ideas of Englishness. Showing the moments at which outsiders used music, literature and film to take centre stage and alter our sense of a sometimes green but sometimes unpleasant land. I in fact start with an Irishman – Oscar Wilde. Collections like this will always have arbitrary parameters, but I see in so many contemporary artists, like Morrissey and Pete Doherty, an artistic mentality that began with Wilde. The cultural upheaval heralded by the Second World War, as anticipated by Evelyn Waugh, carries me into cultural expressions post-World War 2, when the working class were no longer invisible and when women's artistry was no longer so buried, as Shelagh Delaney proved. There was still, to me, something stubbornly class bound about the birth of psychedelia, which I pinpoint to Cambridge University, at the start of a thread which takes me into comedy and post Beyond the Fringe comedians like Stephen Fry and Caroline Aherne. But to me it is Bowie who forms the spine of post-war cultural innovations into identity, with his deeply postmodern approach to artistic personas. He leads me on to Kate Bush, via the innovative sexual plasticity of Lindsay Kemp and then on to the post-punks, with their intellectual insights into identity as concrete and urbanism take hold. Bowie contributed to the opening up of conceptual space within pop which the likes of Jimmy Savile (a disturbing personification of the ineptitude of English institutions to deal with corruption) exploited. Bowie too leads me on to Morrissey, and Brett Anderson (himself informed by William Blake).

In the eighties a cultural episode which Michael Bracewell defined as 'Lipstick and Robots' also heralded the Gothic movement, with The Cure's insights into the stifling emotional terrain of suburbia. New Labour takes us into TFI Friday, the idea of the 'exploded pub' as part of conspicuous public performances of laddishness, with its curious validity of indie rock. The reinvigoration of the nineties led in turn to the reinvigoration of the pop form, as we saw in flashes of glam-rock and in the deeply atmospheric use of textscapes by artists in this decade as inlay cards became textured and pop videos layered with atmospherics. As the dreams of New Labour fade the likes of Tricky document the struggle of artists amongst urbanism, continuing the work of the Manchester post-punks and bringing more racial diversity into over-ground cultural expressions. By the new millennium the economic realities of life for an English artist foster a look into the past in order to find the future (as exemplified by The Long Blondes) and the Dickensian desperation of The Libertines creates a new insight into a fractured land, dotted with violence at bus stops and the occasional arcadian glade. The comedy personas of Johnny Vegas and Stewart Lee nurture humour out of alienation. But amongst an England fragmented by the manifestation of economic choices (and globalisation) artists like Goldfrapp find richness in their appropriation of pagan ideas. If, in the decade we just finished, the likes of Gazelle Twin documented the consequences of a political class focused on economic power then these artists echoed the prescience of writers like JG Ballard by so doing.

England's cultural history is nothing if not reflexive, and I do not pretend that my account can be objective. My subjective take makes about as much sense as a nursery rhyme, with all its childlike cadences and repetitions.

This book was written during a time of acute national unease about the English identity, and this forward was written on the day Britain left the European Union. The political class pushed for a return to a halcyon England, with some of the key players masquerading financial ambition as patriotism. The book ends with me looking to fellow Millennials for a way out of the unease. Perhaps I was reacting to that context through this book's assembly. Though in part the book is a celebration of English culture (at a time during which convincing celebrations about it seem few and far between, for those of us who resisted the charms of the new 50 pence piece) it also takes a frank look at the institutions and collectives that have shaped English culture and the influences they have had. In that respect this book is a polemic. But it is also a tribute to the sheer richness of English culture – what it has reflected in its fragments, what it has shown us of ourselves and what it illuminates. I found that my anger led to introversion out of which was borne fresh idealism. As an author and an Englishman, I found confidence (and pleasure) in rooting around in the treasure box that is English culture, with its sometimes brilliant and its sometimes disturbing contents. I *do* believe passionately in the underrated artistic praxis of PJ Harvey, in the shamanistic qualities of Mark E Smith, just as I earnestly believe that Johnny Vegas' cathartic persona is an underrated source of artistic inspiration. I also believe that Millennials (and I proudly count myself as one) are about to contribute an invigorated chapter to English history, and I look at – frankly under-appreciated – artists like Gazelle Twin to show why.

For me, England's cultural history is a thing of wonder, though my view is not rose-tinted. I have become so aware of the flaws and mistakes of the land that to even wholeheartedly define myself as an Englishman required an act of will. It takes care to not allow ourselves to be appropriated by jingoism or to the momentum of political expedience. My hope is that in reviewing this highly subjective thread that I have pursued, through England's nooks and crannies, you will not only appreciate the artists that have contributed as I did, but also be invigorated once you finish with the past and look to the future.

Guy Mankowski
Lincoln, 31 January 2020

Acknowledgements

I would like to thank my colleagues at Lincoln University – including (but not only) Jason Whittaker, Chris Dows, Catherine Redpath, Dan Pantano and Sue Healy, who offered me a setting in which to undertake investigations and projects like this. I would like to thank all at Zer0 Books for all their work on this publication, in particular John Romans for his kind editing. I thank Roberta Green and Louise Woodcont – themselves brilliant English artists – for their consistent support. I would lastly like to thank my family and offer my gratitude for the support of Vivenne and Andrew Mankowski and for the artistic insights offered by my grandmother, Shirley Firmin.

Chapter 1

Ginger Beer in Teacups, and Leaves on the Lawn – Oscar Wilde, Just William, Sherlock Holmes and The Age of Innocence

The English have always loved a rebel – but only once they have obliterated him.

Oscar Wilde springs to mind. The flamboyant Irishman who was adopted by London would come to find that his decadent lifestyle set him on the road to ruin, as a result of brutality exercised from within the sceptered isle. For all of the charming innocence of the hero of Wilde's *Happy Prince,* there had always been a sense of a threat lacing even his own stories. In *The Happy Prince,* the statue of the late prince is saddened by his view of a town full of starving people. As he is trapped in his own glorious form, he bids a swallow to pluck the jewels from his eyes and give them to the people of the town. Fixed as he may be in his own position, the prince is compelled to help those less fortunate. For all his talents Wilde seemed to retain a soft heart – even when he was rebelling.

Homosexuality was seen as, in the words of Michael Bracewell, 'the worst crime in the English directory of sins'. Evelyn Waugh's brother was expelled from Sherbourne on this charge. It was an exercise in British institutional policing, of the type which also condemned Oscar Wilde. The law would seek to remove the threat of *fin-de-siècle* decadence by imprisoning Wilde. Over the years misguided attempts to 'protect' England would mark it with deep scars, and make it secretive and divided. Force it to maintain a mask of orthodoxy, which remained unconvincing. In centuries to come Wilde would be seen to partly define the charisma of an England that had in fact imprisoned and enslaved him to hard labour. See also the hypocritical largesse of spirit now extended to Alan Turing. By all accounts the Establishment – now so keen to pardon him and put him on bank notes – was exploitative and brutal towards him. You wouldn't know it by all the film adaptations.

Richmal Crompton's impish William, of the beloved *Just William* books, owed his success to the English love of the rebel. Perhaps the English tendency for the young to rebel against the elders can be traced back to the cult around Oscar Wilde. In which case the William books reinvigorated this tendency from 1922 onwards. William and his gang, 'The Outlaws', roleplay as Red Indians, put on dubious museum shows, kidnap visiting dignitaries and get involved in a series of *ostensibly* well-meaning scrapes.

The Just William books are set in the vague boundaries of an idyllic Albion. In *Growing Up with Just William*, Margory Disher suggests that the William stories are set somewhere around Bromley in Kent. You probably don't know where Bromley is – and neither do I – but it sounds quintessentially English, doesn't it? 'Picnics by the motorway in Bromley'. 'A quick stop for cucumber sandwiches in Bromley'. A sign in a Thomas Henry illustration in *William Does His Bit* establishes our hero just north of London. Regardless, Crompton's Edenic England is nestled somewhere in our deep south, with the boundaries of the story porous enough to not feel restrictive. Even if they are as practically inescapable for our protagonist as the village in the late sixties series *The Prisoner* (1967). This seems very much the point – in garnering our affections for William, Crompton is also garnering the reader's affections for a timeless Southern England. A region which, in later decades, Conservative governments would be accused of bias towards when allocating funding. Affection for the south of England – an artistic as well as financial choice.

This is an England of endless summer holidays in which children can roam around the countryside with a free rein, with no fear of paedophiles. It's an England in which older brothers called Robert clumsily attempt to seduce girlfriends under the riverside shade of willows. In which there are older sisters called Ethel and adoring girls-next-door called Joan. There will most likely be no divorce or Tinder for William – at some point he will grow up and he and Joan will live in blissful, stifling matrimony.

This is a world in which William and his Outlaws are always home in time for tea and lashings of ginger beer. Their exuberance never takes them to a place in which their initial position cannot be recovered. England is not a wilderness, except within the consciousness of a childhood game of 'Injuns'. Even when reading these stories as a child with few reference points, I was conscious of the points at which the content of the tales was overshadowed by events of the twentieth century. *William and The Nasties* (our protagonist's attempt to pronounce the term 'The Nazis in the collection *William The Detective*) has him attempt to mimic Nazi storm troopers by driving a Jewish shopkeeper (who Crompton describes in racist terms) from his business. The story, though ultimately anti-Nazi, was removed from the re-published collection but the implications are clear. The real world was bearing down on Crompton's Eden – it was time to wake up. William and his Outlaws, at the end of the story, finally realise there is something very wrong about their attempts to kidnap a shopkeeper because he does not give them extra sweets. The fragile boundaries of their blissful ignorance would soon burst. There was a sense of 'something passing', to quote an observation made by Henry James on the eve of the First World War.

By 1942 another English fictional character, Sherlock Holmes, would also find the porous boundaries of his England tinged by the outside world. In a film adaptation (*Sherlock Holmes and the Voice of Terror*, 1942), Holmes (played by Basil Rathbone) and Watson visit the East End of London. They intend to persuade a lovable moll, named Kitty, to convince her criminal friends to expose a traitor who has been betraying England's military secrets. This film is fascinating because it shows how, at this point in history, the English upper class could still be conceived of as paternal and trusted. Kitty persuades the villains, on Holmes' behalf, to overcome their differences with Scotland Yard in service of a united (you could say One Nation) England. To eject those amongst them that would conspire against our beloved land. In the end, the mob rush out into the night to carry out Holmes' demand. For all the demographic differences between Holmes, Scotland Yard and the criminals there is a sense they are working towards a common cause. England – when pushed – *will* come together.

Holmes was placed by Arthur Conan Doyle in a conceptual space outside of society, which allowed him to traverse its layers at will. It was perhaps a device gleaned from his fascination with the paranormal, where Mediums are not restricted by physical boundaries. As a freelance detective often working in tension with Establishment figure Inspector Lestrade, Holmes was a master of disguise. His ability to change his appearance to blend into any situation in cause of his mission helped him personify the idea of the English eccentric chameleon, in a way that prefigured the likes of David Bowie. But he is not an Übermensch – indeed, the fallibility of the rebel is where his charm originates. In the story *A Study in Scarlet* (1887) his partner Watson summarises Holme's strengths and weaknesses:

1. Knowledge of Literature – nil
2. Knowledge of Philosophy – nil
3. Knowledge of Astronomy – nil
4. Knowledge of Politics – Feeble
5. Knowledge of Botany – Variable. Well up in belladona, opium and poisons generally. Knows nothing of practical gardening
6. Knowledge of Geology – Practical but limited. Tells at a

glance different soils from each other. After walks, has shown me splashes upon his trousers, and told me by their colour and consistence in what part of London he had received them

7. Knowledge of Chemistry – Profound
8. Knowledge of Anatomy – Accurate, but unsystematic
9. Knowledge of Sensational Literature – Immense. He appears to know every detail of every horror perpetrated in the century
10. Plays the violin well
11. Is an expert singlestick player, boxer and swordsman
12. Has a good practical knowledge of British Law

It is worth bearing in mind that this characterisation came from the pen of Arthur Conan Doyle – a medic interested in the occult, able himself to traverse social boundaries. But what Doyle was characterising in Holmes was the English auto-didact, the chameleon as at home in pit fights as in the upper-class environs of an elite secret society. But the tacit admission here is that were Holmes of working-class stock, he would have limited rein. Agency is deeply class bound. Which leads us nicely on to Peter Cook.

Chapter 2

Bedazzled in Soho – from Evelyn Waugh to Shelagh Delaney and Peter Cook

In the English, decadence has always been sanctioned when it has come from the upper classes. There was little overt resistance to the likes of Evelyn Waugh's characters in *Decline and Fall* because they had the cut glass accents and the *decency* to hide their debauchery amongst their lavish interiors. The resistance towards Waugh's characters, in Waugh's novels, comes from the characters themselves, and their own sense of spiritual and moral decay – the outside world offers no boundary. The shells in which the novels are set remain pristine throughout. Whereas Crompton would soft-focus her stories on some region of Kent, Waugh used the idea of the English country home, an organic manifestation of English values, expressed in the 'accumulated art and crystalline architecture of an aristocratic house', to quote Michael Bracewell. In such a setting, a character could safely play out whatever decadences they wished, as long as it was within well-furnished rooms.

Having revelled in the opulence of the English upper classes in *Brideshead Revisited*, Waugh would describe the dawn of a new type of Englishness, in which class boundaries weren't so unbreakable. For all his bloody snootiness, Waugh's disdain of the new England that would emerge was prescient. He was aware that, following the Second World War, England's class boundaries would be traversed. In lieu of a hierarchy of class, materialism would rise as the new ethos. In the final volume of his 'Sword of Honour' collection, entitled *Unconditional Surrender*, Waugh portrayed the figures who would personify this new order. He wrote of a proletariat that 'munched Woolton pies', whilst others 'sucked cigarettes made of sweepings from canteen floors'. After the joint effort to defeat Nazism, the working classes were no longer invisible to the upper classes. They had become a demographic to be reckoned with. But Waugh saw them as lachrymose, driven only by the need to survive. A singular body who 'munched' and 'sucked'– parasitic at worst, anodyne at best. But now British society had been levelled by the war their needs could no longer be dismissed, the pesky proles.

Waugh personifies his dislike of a new classlessness in *Brideshead Revisited* through the character of Captain Hooper. Hooper exemplifies the modern Briton: disdainful of grand homes and gilded lifestyles. The 'something passing' that Henry James noted turned out to be the passing of an ancient tradition. The invisible levers and pulleys of the Old Boys Network would be left to rust. A new democracy would emerge. But where the seeds of a more democratic England might be read, Waugh feared only that the Hoopers of the world were harbingers of dourness, possessing only of 'a profusion of detail about humane legislation and industrial change'. 'Elf and Safety', Waugh feared, would reign as a value system in lieu of the idea of class. Policed, as they frequently had been, by raised noses and withering disdain.

But for all his concerns this would not be an era democratic enough to welcome all. Shelagh Delaney's *A Taste of Honey* was set in her hometown of Salford, and Delaney was driven by the need to see the world she recognised being finally portrayed on the stage. 'I had strong ideas of what I wanted to see on the stage,' she said. 'We used to object to plays where the factory workers came cap in hand and called the boss "sir". Usually North Country people are shown as gormless, whereas in actual fact, they are very alive and cynical.' We can later see this defiance in Mrs Merton, Caroline Aherne's wonderfully acerbic hostess. *A Taste of Honey* would successfully reposition the idea of the working classes as having a voice – and a sharp one at that. Delaney would also be the first to portray the reality of pregnancy on the stage, updating a limited view of modern women that had seen them as either virgins or mothers.

For all the working-class agency that two world wars would permit, working class 'decadence' still retained a whiff of the taboo. This notably changed in the sixties, when youthful rebellion went pop in the form of The Beatles. The comedian Peter Cook – who oozed effortlessly from Radley and then the Cambridge Footlights – became friends with Lennon as his fame peaked. Cook himself would update the idea of the English den of debauchery, from Waugh's country house to the Soho after-hours club. Soho – with its hidden bars, labyrinthine streets and drenched *Englishness*, would be the perfect location for the ironically named Establishment club. In the autumn of 1961 Cook would import ideas he had gleaned from Berlin's nightclubs, and fostered with his friends Nick Luard and John Bird. In the tradition of English rebels who want to rock the boat but certainly not upend it, he told the BBC's *Person to Person* programme in 1979 that he wanted to open a club 'not to change society or to make money', but to find somewhere 'where we could be more outrageous than we could be on stage'. Cook's chosen venue was the Club Tropicana in Soho's Greek Street, an 'All Girl Strip Revue' which had gone bankrupt following that most English establishment of order, the police raid. Luard deemed it the least appealing property he'd ever seen. Cook negotiated the lease.

The significance of the title of the club is worth briefly delighting in. Soho typified anti-Establishment impulses. It was nocturnal, greased by back-handers, and outside the control of Blighty's laws. By 2010, inhabitants of Soho such as Sebastian Horsley would bemoan that 'the air used to be clean and the sex used to be dirty. Now it is the other way round.' Cook soon found that if he wanted his den to work there were plenty of people to pay off. Englanders such as Graham Greene and JB Priestly coughed up the three-guinea membership. All received a pin-up of Harold Macmillan for their trouble – the kind of offering William might have offered for one of his exhibitions. The club was gutted and rebuilt using pine, hessian, steel, glass and black paint to hide all kinds of moral – and actual – dirt. Sean Kenny reconstructed it in a heavily timbered, Tudor-Constructivist style. It would be unfair to characterise the club as a complete departure from the salon-style environs that Waugh's characters, or the Bloomsbury group, might have preferred. Art exhibitions were planned, and it had a cinema club showing free films every afternoon. These films would variously concern the Marx Brothers, Rudolf Valentino and Adolf Hitler. A library of newspapers and journals and a programme of informal lunchtime discussions were programmed, confirming the myth that given the freedom to do anything – even rebel – the English will prefer to basically sip tea and chat.

Cook's administrative headaches were many and varied – from securing the visiting Lenny Bruce heroin to paying-off local gangsters. Each headache was dealt with using copious measurements of English charm, and by exercising a gift for delegation. When Cook found the securement of a parking space impossible he simply parked his car illegally, and let the police tow it to Waterloo every night. Two stagehands were hired to fetch it back for a mere £6 a week. Cook welcomed the police chief who came to eventually chase up the issue like an old friend. Having been poured tea, the charmed policeman enquired about the parking offences. 'Would they by any chance have occurred during the period your American business partner was borrowing your car?' he asked. When Cook confirmed that might have been the case, the policeman instantly deemed the case difficult to trace. 'Scarcely worth the trouble,' he added. It is an exchange one can imagine occurring in a dialogue-heavy Sherlock Holmes story. The gentrified class still had agency, means to circumnavigate the system.

If Cook's ambitions for the club were to generate warmth

rather than heat, his colleague Jonathan Miller fostered darker ideas of rebellion. He wrote an article for *The Observer*, asking *Can English Satire Draw Blood?* He expressed the wish that the club would 'develop the weapons necessary for the final overthrow of the Neo-Gothic stronghold of Victorian good taste'. With an altruistic mind sharpened as a medic in the NHS, Miller was aware of The Establishment's potential. England, he said, was still a country where the posthumous rallying cry 'Theirs not to reason why' represented 'an expression of praise and approval, rather than a signal for a rain of scorching contempt which such blinkered loyalty richly deserved'. The betrayal of England's 'lions, led by donkeys' in the First World War still pulsed through England's psyche. 'It is hoped', said Miller, 'that when The Establishment opens its doors the cry of "Bloody Fools" will ring loud and clear through Soho and down the courtly reaches of Whitehall.'

But Miller was wise enough to know that, just as the Establishment would absorb any threat to its orthodoxy by knighting the likes of rebels like Mick Jagger, so too would the success of this project be 'seriously threatened by a subtle defence with which the members of the (real) Establishment protect themselves against these new attacks'. He spoke, with wisdom, of the 'threat of castration by adoption; of destruction by patronage'. He was right. As Cook said, 'the only blood drawn was from my mouth when somebody hit me round the head with a handbag'.

However, The Establishment wasn't only a playground for the ennobled. Careful observers would have spotted two little known actors propping up the bar – Michael Caine and Terence Stamp. Rebellion *was* becoming less and less the sole concern of the entitled.

Chapter 3

Astronauts of Inner Space – Syd Barrett, Nick Drake and The Birth of Psychedelia

When songwriter Nick Drake auditioned for the Cambridge Footlights he did not fare as well as Cook. The slim, dark-haired singer was not short of prodigious talent, but the Footlights turned him away. But the introspective Drake would not be discouraged for long. He would begin recording his debut album, *Five Leaves Left*, at the tender age of 21, having abandoned Fitzwilliam College mere months short of getting his degree. Whereas Cook would shake off the shackle of a public-school education to thrive at Cambridge, Drake's experience was in stark contrast. Fitzwilliam College is a long way from the image of dreaming spires and silver, winding lakes that mention of Cambridge evoke. Drake's friend Victoria Lloyd recalls, on arriving at Cambridge, Drake 'sitting in his tiny motel-like bedroom' in a 'grim, red-brick building' saying 'it's so awful'. His friend Trevor Dann would recall how lorries coming to the port would 'hang a right past the college, and the windows used to rattle something horrible'. He remembers 'having to put Plasticine round the windows, to stop them shuddering'.

For all its architectural disappointments, Cambridge was fertile creative ground for Drake. It is not hard to see why. Each college is rumoured to have its own ghost. Sir Isaac Newton is reputed to haunt his old rooms at Trinity College where, from his window, he spied the famous apple tree. Clocks are known to stop when no one watches, and books to fall open where no one looks.

Against this rich backdrop, the spirit of enquiry amongst the young was known to bubble into hostility towards the older generation. Yevtushenko's quote 'Do not tell lies to the young' was readily bandied around. Rupert Brooke – the Cambridge educated socialist poet, in his posthumous work 'The Old Vicarage, Grantchester' spoke for all the young men who were butchered at Flanders and on the beaches of Gallipoli. He evocatively described their dreams of dreaming England:

Stands the Church clock at ten to three?
And is there honey still for tea?

Drake was not immune to pastoral reflections on his surroundings, even if he was frustrated by the hidebound nature of the institution. His friend Paul Wheeler recalls Drake playing him the song *River Man*, from *Five Leaves Left*, during his time there. Wheeler noted even then that 'it had an extra dimension to it'.

During his second year, Drake would move into residence in Carlyle Road, by a little bridge, which led on to Jesus Lane. Every time Drake came into town he would cross the river, and Wheeler has long been convinced that this journey would inspire Drake to write his famous *River Man*. In the song, Drake sings of summertime shows which last all night, evoking images of May Balls. With parties spilling out on to the banks which ache all the way down to the River Cam.

The River Cam swirls under the bridges of the colleges, and rushes into a deep bend in the river at a Mill Pond. On the meadows surrounding it Roger Waters and Syd Barrett would play songs for friends on afternoons and weekends. Whilst his contemporary, Nick Drake, drew inspiration from the winding rivers of the city, Barrett's expansive imagination explored the unknown worlds amidst the earthbound riverbank. Syd Barrett's biographer, Julian Palacios, even argued that the 'formative tributaries of psychedelia can be found amongst the sylvan meadows at the Mill Pond'. Evidence of the bucolic and the riverbank as settings in psychedelia can be found decades later on The Verve's *Urban Hymns*, where the LSD-induced otherworldliness of their debut *A Storm In Heaven* was tempered with disciplined melodicism in tracks like *Weeping Willow* and *Catching That Butterfly*.

Given that three members of psychedelic pioneers Pink Floyd (Roger Waters, David Gilmour and Syd Barrett) were students in the scholastic town, you can perhaps see his point. Friends of Barrett even recall him being slightly psychedelic in appearance – dressed in a burgundy, velvet suit with a shock of curly black hair, eyes darkened with eyeliner.

A large back bar, hidden halfway down Cambridge's Market Passage, would see Pink Floyd and Nick Drake drift into the same orbit. The Cri was a popular meeting place for students from the university and the art school. Drake would sit quietly in the corner and the Floyd would drink in there. Where Barrett's songs would concern characters like the dormouse Gerald in *Bike*, Drake's lyrics would also have a psychedelic abstractedness that is often overlooked. In *River Man*, Drake sings of 'going to see the River Man / going to tell him all I can / About the plan / For lilac time'. Drake's personification of the Cam as a man, or perhaps a spirit, and his evocation of a 'lilac time' is comparable to the Floyd's personifications in *Arnold Layne* or *Bike*. As Drake blends time, space and colour into a sensual whole, in *Astronomy Domine* on Floyd's debut, Barrett wrote of 'lime and limpid green / the sounds around / the icy water underground'. The argument could be made that both Drake and Barrett's proximity to the tributaries and lush lawns around the Cam provoked a very English sensibility, containing the essence of psychedelia. An impetus to, in the conceptual space offered by lyrics, create room in which one can exist in a richer, or 'lilac' time.

Barrett's appreciation of Cambridge is apparent in the gorgeously English track *Wined and Dined* which dates back to his university days. In it, he sings of an August garden party he never wants to leave – a lilac time that he longs to preserve.

His haunting vocal captures the melancholic undertow of many student parties, laced as they are with the existential unease of wanting to be at the heart of an occasion which feels all too fleeting, and defined only in retrospect. There is little focus to this charming number; Dave Gilmour added a sinuous sliding lead over Barrett's frazzled vocals, which depicted a twilight event. A party that is lovingly evoked, but which remains out of reach. That quintessential psychedelic blurring of narrative time is there, even in this acoustic, drumless number:

Wined and dined, oh it seemed just like a dream
Girl was so kind.
Kind of love I'd never seen
Only last summer, it's not so long ago
Syd Barrett, *Wined And Dined*

Barrett and Drake's similarities do not end there. Following Barrett's departure from Pink Floyd, he would admit that 'there was an awful lot of trouble'. He added, 'I don't think the Pink Floyd had any trouble, but I had an awful scene, probably self-inflicted, having a Mini and going all over England and things'. With his sensitive psyche bombarded by LSD, DMT and STP – all of which had their own deleterious effects on his mental and physical health – Barrett's withdrawal from the Floyd led to him moving into living space at 101 Cromwell Road. This location was an epicentre for shaky ideas about communal living. Barrett's ex-girlfriend Jenny Spires recalls 101 Cromwell Road as a 'fantastic building ranging over six floors with quite a grand entrance and stairway…large windows on the first two floors with high ceilings, beautiful old sash windows and lovely wide, heavy doorways'. She added that, 'The flat overlooked what must have been a beautiful garden.' One wonders whether members of more recent psychedelic bands such as The Horrors will get to decline in such elegant houses given the rent hikes that followed.

During his own gradual withdrawal, throughout English winters Barrett would drive to far-flung, unknown destinations. Ending up on windswept beaches and wastelands, which would lodge in his psyche and be evoked in his later lyrics.

Crushed by the perceived commercial failure of his albums *Five Leaves Left* and *Bryter Later* (an issue compounded by Drake's complex ambivalence towards the press and to live events) Drake too would see the creativity of his early twenties dissolve along with his withdrawal. Drake would retreat to live with his parents in Tamworth. Like Barrett, Drake would also drive to far-flung destinations, until the oil ran out of his car. Both Barrett and Drake would turn from astronauts of outer space to psychonauts of inner space. Drake's friend Brian Wells talks of Drake driving from Tamworth, saying, 'Nick would come quite late at night, and he'd run out of petrol two miles up the road. He resented going to garages and putting petrol in the car.' As someone who had also experimented with drugs, Drake found the realities of the modern world increasingly objectionable. Drake's father Rodney would describe his journeys across 'tremendous distances' as 'sort of a therapy' for him. Like Barrett, in his later days, Drake would become more and more monosyllabic and withdrawn.

It would be simplistic to say that Barrett's talent simply dropped off following his drug-related trauma. During the latter part of his musical career he developed a greater mastery of his acoustic guitar. As musician John Shamash commented, late 'songs like *Opel* showcase a far more developed ear for dreamy, Lennonesque harmonic twists' [than his earlier work].

But Barrett was irreversibly damaged from breakups with bandmates and girlfriends. The outward-looking psychedelia of *Astronomy Domine* would be replaced with internal dialogues rife with regret. At only 23, Barrett would be looking back over his life. Acoustic songs evoking broken piers, dark globes and fractured quarries litter his late album *The Madcap Laughs*. His mind is no longer concerned with magical beings and outer space, but instead the psychic objects are seashores and borderlines. There is eclecticism to the likes of *Octopus*, in which the very English imageries of his youth eddy and coalesce. We can read in it the influence of Elizabethan sonnets, Edwardian lyrics, Shakespeare, nursery rhymes, eighteenth-century ballads and Victorian travelogues. It is as if all the English references of Barrett's youth became blended, expressed only in the brief, slight format of the song.

Barrett returned to live out his days in Cambridge with his mother, as Drake would return to live out his short life in Tamworth. Both were deeply damaged by drugs and interactions with a world apathetic towards applying ideas about peace and love to reality. But both of them had made impressions on artists who would carry their distinct thread of Englishness on in their own work.

Chapter 4

Velvet Goldmines – David Bowie, Lindsay Kemp and Kate Bush

Astute listeners to David Bowie's early work, such as *The Laughing Gnome*, would have detected the influence of Syd Barrett, whose early lyrical imagery would feature similar magical creatures. Inconvenient then that on hearing Bowie's single *Love You Till Tuesday* during an interview Barrett would dismiss it, saying, 'Yeah, it's a joke number…it's very casual. If you play it a second time it might be even more of a joke. Very chirpy, but I don't think my toes were tapping at all.'

Perhaps Barrett can be forgiven for not taking Bowie too seriously at that moment. At this point in his career, Bowie was a singer who was still finding his identity as an artist. This started to change in 1968, when a secretary in his manager's office sent a copy of Bowie's last album to the actor and dancer Lindsay Kemp. Kemp had been performing, through interpretations of their lives, as Jean Genet, Federico Lorca and, to rejuvenate a thread that glistens throughout England's alternative pop history – Oscar Wilde. Given these figures' brushes with the law regarding their sexuality Kemp had developed a skill for portraying the outsider onstage. He saw something in Bowie, and was enchanted by his vocals. Finding it evocative of Anthony Newley and Jacques Brel, he found in Bowie a 'husky, smoky voice that was plaintive and damaged'. 'I was able to identify with that,' he added; and it is easy to see why.

Kemp started using Bowie's *When I Live My Dream* to open his own shows at The Little Theatre Club off St Martin's Lane. After attending one of his shows, Bowie found himself back at Kemp's flat in Soho. 'My flat was filled with strippers, hookers, pimps and druggies,' Kemp remembers. He notes that Bowie 'looked around, and then he sat down – and was completely at home'.

If Bowie hadn't yet fully styled his voice as an outsider, he was certainly comfortable with them, as his fascination with Lou Reed, Iggy Pop and Andy Warhol's Factory scene would later prove.

With a sailor father who'd been lost at sea and a mother who had encouraged him to dress up and wear makeup, Kemp had developed, seemingly through force of will, a distinct blend of drag, mime, song and dance. He had, as a result, become a deeply respected dance teacher. As Bowie and Kemp drew closer they enthusiastically revelled in a shared love of music hall, Oriental and ritualistic theatre, Kabuki and The Theatre of the Absurd. As a result Kemp helped add to Bowie's repertoire, in his words, a 'desire to move'. The Oriental and Kabuki element would soon become apparent in the persona with which Bowie would finally find fame. That of a Martian rock star called Ziggy Stardust, backed by his Spiders from Mars. More importantly, Ziggy would allow Bowie to present the persona of an ultimate outsider – an alien. Taking cues from Kemp's performances of outsiders Bowie was able to take this metaphor to the extreme, and embody it until it provoked a personal identity crisis.

In 1976, having seen an advert for Lindsay Kemp's show *Flowers*, a young Kate Bush would be drawn in by the advert's promise to show people how to 'live fabulously through your senses'. Bush recognised the power of a performance in which someone would offer themselves through music, whilst also giving themselves physically. Attending Kemp's classes, she soon expanded her repertoire with expansive arm movements and rich facial expressions, which became useful in her expressive video for her debut single *Wuthering Heights*. Inspired by a BBC adaptation of Emily Brontë's novel the song sees Bush use lines from the character Catherine Earnshaw, pleading at Heathcliff's window to be let in. But Catherine is in fact a ghost. In this song, English texts from the past, adapted for TV, were themselves haunted *by* Bush, in order to portray a haunting.

Bowie's own alternative visions came to the fore amongst the fertile breeding ground that was Haddon Hall. A decaying Victoria mansion in Beckenham, complete with turrets, Gothic stained-glass windows and a banqueting hall, it became the hub at which the Ziggy persona was work-shopped full-time. It was bankrolled by Bowie's manager Ken Pitt, along with the proceeds from the hit *Space Oddity.* Woody Woodmansey and Trevor Bolder would be recruited to Haddon to play drums and bass. The rhythm section of the Spiders from Mars would sleep on mattresses on the house's expansive balcony. They would join producer Tony Visconti and his girlfriend Liz, who would take the back bedroom on the ground floor. Sharing a huge living room with David and Angie Bowie, Visconti would persuade the owner of the house (apparently a Mr Hoys) to let him build a rehearsal space in its wine cellar. In this lavish new court Bowie was King and Angie Queen. It was a space that would become an unofficial demo studio, a photo-shoot location, a campaign office and a Ziggy commune. A geographic space in which Bowie's meditations, impulses and ambitions would flourish. A velvet goldmine, in which lavish and quintessentially English ideas would be fleshed out, making all involved famous.

In styling himself as an alien commenting on England – in songs such as *Five Years* – Bowie offered not just sharp outsider commentary on the state of the nation but also the possibility of *escape.* As Dick Hebdige argued, 'Bowie's meta-message was escape – from class, from sex, from personality, from obvious commitment – into a fantasy past...or a science-fiction future.' It is unbelievably impressive how many alternative modes of living Bowie created in his various allusions and depictions. As Sheila Whiteley argued, 'Rock, then, may be viewed as a fin-of-this-siècle bourgeois bohemia, in that it provides opportunities to figuratively step "outside" bourgeois life.' Bowie had already been bold enough to step outside the hard structure of English life at that time with his artistic living arrangements. Through the Ziggy persona he would soon be inspiring his listeners to do the same. His voice would remind us that he was one of us, whilst his dress would tell us that he was one of *them*. The sense of fluidity with which he expressed a sense of possibility was charismatic and inspired others to undertake such transitions.

Chapter 5

Disco Lento and The New Europeans – Depeche Mode, Ultravox and Hurts

Bowie's later stylings would see him start to look beyond England. Bowie described how, post Ziggy, he created the hugely influential album *Low* as a response to 'seeing the Eastern Bloc [of Europe], how East Berlin survives in the midst of it'. But he felt unable to articulate this landscape in words, saying 'it was something that...required textures'. These textures found themselves represented on both sides of *Low*.

Side one contained fragmented, synth-drenched songs, decorated with Carlos Alomar's guitar, which were at once concise and exploratory. Side two held desolate instrumentals, broken with freeform vocals that cut straight to the marrow. In her book *Poor But Sexy: Culture Clashes, Europe East and West*, Agata Pyzik accurately describes *Low* as a 'psycho-geographic' album on which Bowie mapped his inner landscapes. Caught in the clutches of cocaine psychosis, Bowie had fled to Berlin to detox, with Iggy Pop in tow, where he made *Low*. He was greeted with a strange, dislocated city: the empty shells of deserted housing and the ruins of war. Each of the two component blocs were deprived of information about the other. They therefore became blank canvases for the wheeling imagination, both for Germans and non-Germans.

The post-punks – for whom *Low* was massive – were deeply preoccupied by Eastern Europe in general. Pyzik writes of 'the post-punk Bowiephile obsession with the Eastern Bloc': an encapsulation so neat that it renders an abstract set of ideas readily applicable. Pyzik elaborated, saying: 'For the mythology of post-punk...three cities only really mattered.' In her words 'The Berlin-Warszawa-Moscow express used to map the phantasmagorical geography of the Eastern Europe of the mind, made in equal parts of ashes and brocade, death and glamour.' The harsh aesthetics of the ruin, check-point and brocade were indeed attractive to post-punks.

Bands such as Basildon's Depeche Mode mined Eastern European aesthetics very carefully. In band photos they were often captured standing in severe black coats against very European-looking pillars. The video for their single *Everything Counts* carefully balanced Eastern and Western aesthetics. On the one hand, they sang stacked shoulder to soldier like East German soldiers on parade (even if their haircuts were probably too daft to pass even the most liberal military standard). On the other hand, the camera flitted admiringly over skyscrapers and flyovers, as if in praise of Western capitalism and its sleek edifices. Depeche Mode sang of how 'your handshake seals the contract / On the contract there's no turning back' – unconsciously predicting the hyper-capitalism that would surge in Eastern Europe in the years that followed. It was a balancing act that managed to appeal to the youth in East and West Europe, but for very different reasons. In Sascha Lange's book on the band, *Monument*, she describes how, 'for East German teenagers, Depeche Mode opened up a cosmos of endless yearning...for material goods not available on the East German market – posters, records, magazines'. But Western audiences, too, found the appropriation of an Eastern aesthetic appealing. Other post-punks, such as Ultravox, made albums full of 'angry exclamations of fear and loathing for Western civilisation', such as *Ha Ha Ha*.

The 'glamour' component of the equation Pyzik refers to is perhaps most forcibly present in Ultravox's *Vienna* encapsulating as it does the post-punk glamourisation of Europe. The smoke-swept video to this song (recorded in fact as much in Covent Garden as during a snatched, budget trip to Vienna) attempts to capture the decadent, European opulence of an embassy party.

Like many enduring pieces of contemporary art, it sticks in the consciousness as much for its failures as for its successes. The embassy party scene was filmed in a rented accommodation in North London. In it, candles and chandeliers light a room in which elegant guests are dressed in a curious mix of clothing. The outfits range from high society evening-wear to Blitz Club era New Romantic garb. Veils, long gloves, fur and feather boas abound, whirling against a backdrop of expansive staircases. Confidantes whisper in the ears of severe, monocle-wearing diplomats, and it is all very creepy and unnerving. In retrospect the video is not as enchanting as it could have been, with it now mainly evoking the 1993 Ferrero Rocher advert – famously housed at the mysterious 'ambassador's reception'.

The album that accompanied *Vienna* on its cover photo hinted at a 'post-punk uniform', which other bands such as Orange Juice adopted in this era. This uniform was comprised of the sharp blazer, the fastened top button and the side-parting – with eyeliner an optional extra. Photos portrayed a young aesthete, deeply preoccupied with a matter just out of shot, eyes fixed on some real or conceptual European horizon. The album's song *New Europeans* suggested that the mysterious realm over-the-water was being viewed in aspirational terms.

This enthralment was potent enough to still be evident in pop videos decades later. The Manchester synth-pop band Hurts deftly created a European mythology of their own with their debut video for the single *Wonderful Life*. Within 4 minutes they created an evocative visual landscape, rich with reference points, which proved that even in the contemporary era Europe retained a sense of mystique for the English. This admiration was apparent in everything from the lone dancer, dressed like an extra from a Berlin Cabaret, to a backdrop evoking a continental art school. By the time the final, aching saxophone (straight out of a Tears for Fears single) wailed its long notes the message was clear; we are New Europeans.

In interviews regarding their formation the duo described a desperate trip to Italy in which they discovered the sounds of Disco Lento, a genre of music concerned apparently with 'slow, electronic ballads'. Disco Lento seems as wispy and attractive as the band's aesthetic – try to pin down exactly what it is and it slips through your fingers. The Wikipedia page that once existed for this genre has long vanished, making Disco Lento a physical and digital ghost.

It goes without saying that the Europe of this phantasmagoria did not exist. It was a snatched vision, its content altered by attempts to capture it. These stylised European visions then became an assumed reality of their own, even if, in the real world, they never became a physical zone. But this vision had within it a strong enough core for artists to call and respond with it at will. There is, doubtless, a conceptual strength here permanent enough to endure across various artistic ventures and still connect with audiences. The unfamiliar may be party to these evocations and assume that somewhere, they can be lived-in. These visions might be useful as analogues, projections that are illustrative of emotions evoked, and the provocations behind them. But perhaps where such a vision is most useful is in how they encourage other artists to make their own creative visions as full-blooded as possible.

Chapter 6

Catching That Butterfly – Alan Sillitoe, Paul Weller and Liza Radley

Where David Bowie would style himself as an alien, writing lyrics deep-rooted in seventies England, Paul Weller would always style himself as recognisably English. Between 1978 and 1982 Weller's lyrics would portray an Albion that his listeners recognised only too well. Far from simply penning mundane descriptions of the land, his words contained striking insights into the human condition and the construction of English society.

In the 1980 song *Going Underground* Weller's anger was directed at a political class that prioritised weapons over care:

You choose your leaders and place your trust
As their lies wash you down and their promises rust
You'll see kidney machines replaced by rockets and guns

But on the single's B-side, *Tales From The Riverbank*, Weller painted a more abstract picture in a song where he depicts solace as not coming from the ruling class, but from the land itself. 'This is a tale from the water meadows,' he sings, adding that he is 'trying to spread some hope into your heart'. But Weller seems aware that finding comfort in the terrain of *The Wind in The Willows* might seem regressive. 'True it's a dream mixed with nostalgia,' he sings, 'But it's a dream I'll always hang onto.' With the line 'Won't you join me by the riverbank?' he seems to invite the listener into this reverie, into this soothing space, along with him.

On the album *Sound Affects*, a sense of home is examined through the character of Liza Radley. 'All the people in the town where we live say she's not quite right,' he sings, his empathy apparent when he adds, 'She don't fit in with a small town.' So how does this Liza deal with her sense of isolation? She kisses the face of someone looking on, and declares that 'life means nothing at all'. This could be interpreted as affection and defiance, where one might have expected anger. Weller's palette had more colours in it than people might credit – he was not merely raging against the machine.

Following The Jam's success, Weller would revel in the room he had to explore his thematic preoccupations more deeply. He would become increasingly engaged with the poetry wing of the publisher *Riot Stories*. His poem *In The Summer Months* is striking for showing a more bucolic, pastoral side to his view of England, which The Jam's lyrics might not have readily revealed. *In The Summer Months* is a tribute to England's sun-kissed days, to hours spent 'boating on a lazy river' and to afternoons 'butterfly catching with nets'. The track had a languor that some might not have expected from a performer as wired as he often appeared to be. In the poem, Weller writes of holding up hands 'to see the sun and see through ourselves', suggesting that in England's natural settings a clarity about mankind can be reached. In *Tonight at Noon* lines about the 'volatile world of yesterday' suggest too Weller is all too aware of the transience of any Albion-based utopia, given the country's painful past.

Weller would frequently cite the works of Allan Sillitoe as an influence, in particular his much-vaunted novel *The Loneliness of The Long-Distance Runner*. Weller stated his sense of identification with 'the character in *Saturday Night, Sunday Morning*' in a 1979 interview. 'He knows that everything is going against him,' Weller said, 'and he realises there is nothing you can do about it, but there's obviously something inside him that says, "they're never going to make me change" and "I'll always think this way" and that's all you can do'. Insightfully, he added – 'that's pretty much how I feel'. These observations are arguably still relevant today, given a push towards Brexit that many of the young do not identify with.

Weller's quote offers a compelling insight into how he would psychologically deal with his ongoing sense of rebellion. Where Peter Cook dismissed the idea of rebellion Weller would rage against the dying of the light. Insisting quietly to himself that, as a poet with a developed inner world – a king of infinite space – he would acknowledge all around him but not falter within himself.

Chapter 7

Interzones, Edgelands, Psykick Dancehalls and Shamans – Gary Numan, Joy Division and Mark E Smith

Given their willingness to 'step outside' the norm, in looking for influences, the post-punks of the late 1970s and early 1980s carried on a tradition first established by Bowie. Gary Numan, singer in the band *Tubeway Army*, wore his debt to Bowie openly – even brazenly – by presenting himself in alien form. With inhumanly pale white skin and hair, and with a uniform composed of severe black office wear, he was one of us and yet he was not. An embodiment of what Freud called the unheimlich – the unhomely and the strangely familiar. In pop music the power of the unheimlich seems to be in presenting us with a familiar figure – the office worker – and making them somehow unnerving. Our values, or sense of reality even, are then thrown into question through this confrontation. For this, Numan was perhaps more innovative than he was credited as being.

But Numan did not just want to unnerve us and leave it at that. He had more disturbing visions he wanted us to turn our attention to. Whereas the Ziggy Stardust album was sketchy regarding its dystopian visions, *Tubeway Army's* lyrics concerned a future metropolis with a little more detail. In it, 'Machmen' were androids with cloned human skin controlling the population under the orders of officials dubbed 'Grey Men'. Amidst the increasing urbanity of the late seventies, with the failure of Brutalist architecture to offer much more than isolation and dread, the idea of 'alienation' became more and more prevalent. We *were* alienated – from all sorts of promises that the modern world had offered. The promises of the Fordist, social democratic and industrial world all lay in tatters. A neo-liberal and – crucially – consumerist age was emerging.

Other bands of this era, such as Joy Division, also reflected the alienating effects of their urban surroundings in their work. The academic Giacomo Bottà argues that an 'innovation at the level of cultural sensibility' led to the reconceptualisation of place during the post-punk movement, which began at this point. This reconceptualisation permitted musicians to claim urban zones for themselves, as areas in which they could foster an identity and express their inner world. Bottà argues that:

> Punk scenes in industrial cities were able to rearticulate the private vacant industrial spaces, into public ones, both materially (by gathering in them) and at the imaginary level (by using them in pictures, lyrics).

Bottà's conceptualisation of the different ways in which artists express themselves and form their identity uses ideas of 'articulation' that were first deftly proposed by Stuart Hall. In the words of Hall, articulation is 'a linkage between that articulated discourse and the social forces which it can...but need not necessarily, be connected'. Bottà built upon this idea of 'articulation', using it as a term by which to explore how an artist can express themselves and disseminate their work in three 'dimensions'. Bottà posited that 'territorialisation through music occurs in...textscapes, landscapes and soundscapes', writing:

> The lyrics and titles of songs make up a band's textscapes. The use of local music tradition, local vernacular, or typical city noises constitutes a bands soundscape. Finally the landscape covers all the visual elements.

He considered the work of post-punk artists in relation to these 'articulations'. Bottà analysed the work of Joy Division within the context of their particular creative milieu, taking into account the grim socio-economic conditions that prevailed in Manchester during the eighties. In particular, he wrote of how, 'in their lyrics the built environment is evoked because of its monotony and desolation, structuring a sinister textscape, which only through circulation may be identified as Manchester by listeners'.

Bottà's work contextualised these practices within the harsh socio-cultural backdrop of neo-liberal politics advocated at the time by Margaret Thatcher. Bottà argued that the economic policies of Thatcher (in which individual entrepreneurialism was strongly favoured over community investment) actually gave rise to the bleak, desolate urban spaces that post-punks would draw into their work. Bottà describes how undeveloped urban spaces were, ironically enough, fertile ground for post-punk, writing that the 'lack of identity and direction during the crisis (of the eighties recession) reveal[ed] the citizens' attempts to dramatize their own condition sonically and occupy city spaces with speed and noise'. This is what markedly happened during post-punk.

The architectural theorist Owen Hatherley brought a different perspective to Bottà's analysis. Hatherley argued that there was a 'delayed cultural reaction' to sudden urban developments in cities like Manchester, which were rebuilt in the 1960s but whose effect 'only registered 10 years later when punk claimed towers and walkways as home in places like Hulme Crescents'. Hatherley described how 'post-punk is usually represented in grim towers and blasted wastelands. Places which survive in fragments outside the ring road.' The link between these alienated urban spaces (which convey a bleak sense of the fragmentary) and the post-punk movement was richly evoked in John Foxx's 1980 video for *Underpass*. In it, Foxx appropriated inner city walkways and underpasses within his identity, situating himself amongst them during the act of performance. Architectural visions of utopian new complexes would no longer convince. Artists had been left to claim the wreckage and rubble as their own.

Many post-punk artists from Joy Division's era were residents of Manchester's Hulme Crescents, a Brutalism housing complex. A 1975 survey documenting the personal experiences of urban life in the Crescents found that, far from living utopian lives, 96.3 per cent of tenants wanted to leave. It stated:

> Many people suffer from loneliness, depression and anxiety, finding the estate an intimidating place in which to live. Worry about street crime, drug abuse and break-ins makes many people, particularly women and elderly people, shut themselves up in their homes.
> Fraser, cited in Bottà (2005).

Given the intense urban regeneration during the 1980s it is unsurprising that many post-punk musicians expressed a sense of alienation in their work. Indeed, conveying a sense of 'alienation' through the visual landscapes they were pictured amongst could be considered part of Joy Division's idiosyncratic 'landscape', to use Bottà's definitions.

Kevin Cummins took perhaps the most well-known images of Joy Division, capturing them on Manchester's snow-covered Princess Parkway. In line with the negation and fragmentation inherent to their music in these images the band appear remote. They look alienated and polarised – even within what was their own milieu.

Elsewhere Cummins photographed the band against a backdrop of high-rise buildings and tower blocks. Amongst architectural sites, formed as a result of the socio-political situation Bottà described, intended as affordable, highly functional living spaces.

Andy Beckett summarises well the music of this era in his book *When the Lights Went Out*, writing, 'if Manchester music has a legendary sound, it is the empty-factory echo of Joy Division'. Beckett deftly linked the reverb-laden sound of Joy Division to the empty factories of their city, echoing with neglect. As Dave Haslam noted in Beckett's book, 'it seemed as if the bleakness of the failed landscape around them was seeping into their music'.

Jon Savage eloquently wrote how Joy Division's work evoked Manchester during this era. He wrote that 'Joy Division's spatial, circular themes and Martin Hannett's shiny, waking-dream production gloss are one perfect reflection of Manchester's dark spaces and empty places: endless sodium lights and hidden semis seen from a speeding car, vacant industrial sites – the endless detritus of the nineteenth century'. The brutal force of Thatcher's social change had acted like a kind of industrial wind tunnel, kicking up the dust of England past and forcing us to live in its miasma. Aside from the evocations related to a speeding car, Savage is here referring to how, during this era, artists were finding an aesthetic home in the 'dark spaces and empty places' despite (or perhaps because of) a lack of physical room in which artists could explore their ideas.

This portrayal of alienation was consistent with Joy Division's lyrics. In the song *Interzone* Ian Curtis sings of how he 'walked through the city limits / trying to find a clue / trying to find a way to get out'. To Curtis the city is a site of unbearable negation, which must be escaped, or within which new living space must be found. This new space, Curtis hopes, will 'yield a clue', presumably towards the way out of an urban labyrinth, and to his own survival. Bottà describes the 'depersonalized space and monotonous urban landscape' evident in Joy Division's work, a condition that we now know Curtis dearly wanted to escape. It is only in retrospect that the articulacy of his articulations are apparent.

Elsewhere in his oeuvre, Curtis' *lack* of articulacy would be compelling. His onstage performances – in which jerky, robotic movement would become indiscernible from the epileptic fits he suffered – seemed to channel a very real sense of abandon. It was almost as if Curtis was channelling chaotic, angry spirits.

Marshalling the fury of the audience and making himself totemic in the process. Mark Fisher described Joy Division as 'unwitting necromancers who had stumbled on a formula for channelling voices' and his description seems most applicable to Curtis. Curtis was both otherworldly and yet, unlike Bowie, he was not suggesting this 'other' was a better place to be. In fact, his lyrics sometimes suggested a man who had seen other eras and had found them just as brutal, if not more brutal, than our own. We could, decades later, see evidence of the frontman standing as representative for the angst of their audience in the cult around Teesside band The Chapman Family on the onstage self-flagellation of their frontman, Kingsley Chapman.

Manchester, for all its urbanity, retains this sense of the otherworldly in its subculture. With their removed performance styles Ian Curtis and Mark E Smith seemed to act as totems on this unseen energy grid, necromancers or shamans in the mould of Jim Morrison. Whether in the grinding, industrial pull of The Fall's *Reformation* or in Joy Division's soundscapes there is a sense of some dark magic being summoned by industrial repetition, evoking as it does the working practices of the city and the compulsive need to escape into the otherworldly. One only has to dance in late night indie discos, housed in spooky buildings like Manchester's Star and Garter, to get a sense that they are sat on powerful ley lines, with the city's industrial practices sitting on the over-ground, sparking and igniting on top of much more powerful, unseen undercurrents.

Artistic collectives like Salford's The White Hotel and Newcastle's The Candy Vortex seem to respond to such unacknowledged cultural undercurrents, with participants in each 'scene' performing as characters who respond to these unspecified energies. The White Hotel would attract tabloid attention with their re-enactment of Princess Diana's funeral with staged 'mourners', as if using the idea of a public spectacle to acknowledge a powerful phenomenon that had affected the country. In the words of organiser Austin Collings, they used this event (complete with Tony Blair impersonators) as they were 'essentially telling an absurd story of class, monarchy, racism and corruption'. The Candy Vortex (whose aesthetic combined *The Valley of the Dolls* with that of a cheap horror film to achieve a Rimbaudian derangement of the senses) would encourage participants to dress up as characters from films or in the guise of their private artistic personas during events, where they could similarly express themselves in ways that normative life would not allow.

One can only wonder what would happen if the underground and over-ground combined, and the likes of Curtis seemed crushingly familiar with both. As Mark E Smith sang, in The Fall's *Psykick Dancehall*, 'the vibrations will live on'. (As a self-professed psychic and tarot card reader, Smith was familiar with such concepts and terms.) Mark E Smith, Ian Curtis and Tricky are perhaps the only contemporary 'frontmen' who expressed themselves with such spontaneous idiosyncrasy onstage. It seems no coincidence that their music comprised lots of rhythm and repetition. Mark E Smith frequently voiced the opinion that repetition was discipline, and in tracks like *Reformation* the discipline shown by the musicians seems about more than the word 'discipline' would implicate. It is almost as if within this discipline these artists fostered in themselves, and the listener, a kind of spiritual practice which allowed them to tunnel deeper into the songs, into their essence. In Tricky's music the loops would have a glossy, R&B texture, and in The Fall and Joy Division a far more industrial grind. On Joy Division's *Disorder* (from *Unknown Pleasures*) our protagonist is 'walking through the city limits'. Given the urban subject matter of these vocalists, the repetitive nature of their backing music and the idiosyncrasy of their performances it appears as if (perhaps unbeknownst to the singers) their praxis is consumed with some kind of ritualistic unveiling of the layers of consciousness, and by extension the geographic layers of the places that their songs depict. Dr Stanley Krippner analysed Jim Morrison's approach to performing and concluded that in his clumsy appropriation of shamanistic techniques he was a 'failed shaman'. In Krippner's words, 'disciplined use of altered states of consciousness' – as might be achieved through loud and confrontational music repeated – is required for a shaman to be successful. There is arguably much overlap between the role of the frontperson and the shaman anyway. In Krippner's words, 'like traditional shamans, artists have communities that look to them for guidance'.

Surviving recordings, in which Joy Division guitarist Bernard Sumner hypnotised Ian Curtis, reinforce this sense of the otherworldly. In these recordings Sumner regressed Curtis to a previous life. Curtis talked of having travelled 'far and wide through many different times'. It is possible that whatever subconscious vaults he was accessing in these recordings – if we are to take them seriously – he also accessed in his lyrics. The otherworldly is less 'somewhere else' but more a sense of the 'other' within the crushingly familiar urban present. *Mr Pharmacist* (from *Bend Sinister*) is about escape through chemical derangement, a theme that would also emerge in Suede's early work. If the city has a subconscious, such artists seem to be accessing it, as well as their own.

In Curtis' descriptions of stupid, venal politicians (in *Leaders of Men*) and the idiocy of war (*Walked In Line*), it almost seems that Curtis was anticipating, through artistic engagement with his subconscious, future wars. If Carl Jung is to be believed the subconscious is our path to the collective unconscious, in which universal truths can be accessed. In particular Curtis' lyrics on these songs bring to mind the ignored mass protests against the Iraq War which would disempower the youth and make them feel that even in a democracy their voice was irrelevant. Perhaps it was just mindfulness of the Second World War, given Curtis' interest in Nazism, that was informing his lyrics. Regardless, it is only in retrospect that Curtis' chronicling of the changing cityscape seems particularly prescient. Regardless, the use of the subconscious in lyric writing (if only through the lyricist not *consciously* crafting them) could be the beginning of a praxis that leads to lyrics that are richly prescient. Mark E Smith would be credited with having predicted, in his lyrics, the bombing of the Manchester Arndale Centre and the kidnapping of Terry Waite (*Terry Waite Sez* from the album *Bend Sinister*). What at the time might have seemed a careless approach to his music given the unfurling of events on the world stage in retrospect seems far more interesting, not least in the results of his collaborative approach. Mark E Smith's former partner, Brix Smith, would write in her biography:

I believe that Mark is a psychic. He's written songs about things that came to pass later. I am quite a spiritual person. I also believe that I'm a psychic. I believe that he and I connect on multi levels. I believe that everything is vibrational based. We could talk about that all day. I hear things in my head. I'm not nuts. Maybe I am nuts. (Laughs). Where does inspiration come from? You tell me. I hear in my head this song is called Terry Waite Sez. I hand the song to Mark. I tell him it HAS to be called Terry Waite Sez. At this point Terry Waite was the envoy to the Archbishop of Canterbury. We record the song. He ends up getting kidnapped. The song is released. Then his family call Beggars Banquet record company. They believe there might be clues in the lyrics as to where he's being held. That was one instance but there were many more.
Brix Smith, The Rise, The Fall and The Rise

In 1984 The Pet Shop Boys would show how even in the capital city's West End the pressure of inner-city living was overwhelming. Neil Tennant addresses an urban protagonist in the song, singing:

You think you're mad
Too unstable
Kicking in chairs and knocking down tables
In a restaurant in a West End town
Call the police
There's a madman around
The Pet Shop Boys, West End Girls

But where Curtis would 'try to find a way to get out', Neil Tennant would find refuge 'in a dive bar, in a West end town'. The pop idea of a decadent underworld as a place of refuge would prove to be alive and well in 1984. But whereas Curtis was trying to escape the unbearable negation of an 'Interzone', in London it would be the proliferation of lifestyle choices that would unnerve Tennant, who sang:

Too many shadows whispering voices
Faces on posters too many choices
If when why what?
How much have you got?
Have you got it?
Do you get it?
If so how often?
Which do you choose
A hard or soft option?
The Pet Shop Boys, West End Girls

Just as Curtis portrayed the brutal reality of life in an underfunded North, Tennant portrayed the overpowering pressure of choice in the capital city.

Chapter 8

Beyond the Boundaries of Pop and Rebellion – The Jimmy Savile Scandal

If David Bowie used pop music to represent the possibility of escape, and the likes of Curtis were haunted by these ideas, the now disgraced DJ Jimmy Savile ruthlessly exploited those who had stepped outside. In retrospect there is scant sense that he was 'stepping outside' normative life in a way that was intended to benefit others, as some pop figures had. Throughout his lifetime the charity fund-raiser and TV personality developed a lifestyle that enabled him to live outside the legal and domestic paradigms England often takes for granted. Though many would enquire how a man managed to become so ubiquitous and yet so elusive the lack of satisfying explanation renders Savile a kind of contemporary bogeyman.

The fact that police investigations into his serial sexual offences never resulted in any convictions allows Savile to figuratively haunt contemporary culture. The way that the Establishment has surgically removed mentions of a figure prominent enough to feature in everything from *Top of the Pops* to *Tweenies* suggests a country still reeling from the real and conceptual abuse Savile inflicted. Having been cited as one of Britain's most prolific sex offenders, the fact that Savile's Wikipedia page has a section marked 'Aftermath' seems apt. Savile's abuse – of institutions, of trust, of children and vulnerable people – make him epiphenomenal. He has so affected England's perception of itself, and who it can trust, that he is almost too huge a figure to contemplate with any objectivity, too pervasive a figure to be captured in written reflection. Or as some neat digression in a narrative. Subsequent enquiries into Savile have used the thin balm of objective prose to conclude that abuse of his kind could not occur again. But since when could the lexis of aloof bureaucratic language convincingly capture the very corporeal invasions he was guilty of?

As Mark Fisher wrote (in his own consideration of Savile within the context of contemporary culture), in Savile's case it was as if 'the sheer implausibility of corruption and abuse itself form[ed] a kind of cloak for the abuser; *surely this can't be happening?*' Reality is shaped by the convictions of the confident given that reality has no tacit objectivity. Savile was aware that the timid and vulnerable lacked the confidence to shape their sense of reality, and that they would look externally for validation. Savile used trusted institutions – from the BBC to Stoke Mandeville Hospital – to prey on innocent people. The fact that his abuse was not prevented until long after he died threw a dark new light on England's relationship with institutions and celebrities. Savile offers a grave cautionary tale of what happens when famous figures are given (quite literally in the case of Stoke Mandeville) keys to British institutions, on the premise that they are so familiar and engaging that they can't be dangerous. Savile's victims must have thought, as Fisher wrote, 'this can't be happening'.

This grotesque sense of the surreal was the emotional zone that Savile keenly occupied. He was aware, as so many abusers are, that enough force of will overpowers people who are less sure, and if people are unsure of their place within an institution, they will endure a lot rather than risk it. As Fisher wrote, 'Consensual reality, the common-sense world that we like to think we live in, wasn't adequate to a figure like Savile.' It is almost as if he was testing the boundaries of reality, using shock and the confidence of the entitled to traverse social and legal boundaries at will. 'I don't have to do anything,' Savile once said. 'I just have to be. I'm like a piece of soap in the bath; you can see it but when you try to get hold of it its gone.' It seems disgustingly ironic that the ephemeral medium of pop music was exploited by one ephemeral enough to evade justice. Key features of Savile's abuse were that it frequently took place in fleeting settings, such as his caravan, and that he carefully engineered relationships with our gatekeepers of reality – such as the police force – to enable him to dismiss any accusation. Three police forces received complaints about Savile, and all dismissed them. His charity work enabled him to 'officially' maintain the guise of a good person. It is curious how pop music offers an opportunity to 'step outside' normative life but how it still sits within an overarching consensus of the type Fisher deftly described.

Part of the problem was the sheer ephemerality of the pop landscape Savile situated himself in. The backstage parties and late-night dancehalls in which he made a name for himself were the few places in which the bohemian escaped the strictures of normative life and the legal boundaries that usually reinforced it. Savile stated that he knew that 'young girls don't gather round me because of me – it's because I know the people they love, the stars…I am of no interest to them'. His awareness of his place within the fluid, temporary and aspirational systems of the pop world allowed him to forensically exploit it.

It is telling that the one occasion when Savile was reprimanded for his abuse was on the bounded setting of the luxury liner the SS Canberra. Savile had attempted to lure a 14-year-old girl into his cabin, and the girl escaped abuse only because a friend, who took photos of the incident, was present. The parents of the girl complained to a ship's officer that the 51-year-old celebrity had been pursuing their daughter around the ship. A few days later Savile was summoned to the ship's captain. The captain later said, 'I told Savile he disgusted me and I wanted him off my ship when we reached Gibraltar. I detailed an officer to make sure he remained in his cabin until we reached the rock. He was to take all his meals in the cabin and he was not allowed to leave it under any circumstances short of a shipwreck.' Unable to flee in a camper van or elude accusation through duped authority figures Savile had to meekly accept the reprimand. Once unleashed back into society Savile would continue to offend.

With an abuser's eye for an opportunity, Savile exploited the contemporary freedoms offered by the era. It is possible that Savile was passing on the mental paradigm regarding sex that he'd been impressed with as a child. In his autobiography he described losing his virginity to a young woman who picked him up in a dancehall. He described his feelings as 'terror mixed with embarrassment' when the woman slipped her hand into his trousers before attempting to have sex with him on a train, before she 'took what she wanted' in a bush at the back of her house.

It is unnerving, when reading reports from Savile's victims, how much their accounts echo the use of opportune, often public scenarios like the one Savile described. This begs the question of whether Savile was projecting into his victims the feeling of terror and embarrassment he had felt when assaulted. But there seemed to be an even deeper pathology at play. Psychiatrist Oliver James, having interviewed Savile, concluded that he possessed a dark triad of personality traits – Machiavellianism, psychopathy and narcissism. Staff at Broadmoor Hospital certainly held the view that Savile was a paedophile with a personality disorder. Health minister Edwina Currie, who signed off his appointment to a taskforce at Broadmoor, later proved Savile's Machiavellianism when she stated that he had 'a hold' over staff in the hospital given information he retained on them. In bounded environments that he could not escape from he ensured control through information.

When Savile asked himself, in an autobiography chapter titled 'What Shall I Say At the Pearly Gates and at the Judgement Table', he answered, with the confidence of the brazen, that if St Peter pointed out all the sins he had committed he would argue that it was 'the machine of [his] body that had caused him to do such things'.

But there is a wider historical context. As Deborah Orr wrote, 'Savile exploited the chaos created by changing attitudes – to sex, class, youth, culture, entertainment, money, fame – even to public services and charity – that were themselves a response to an industrial age of rapid technological advancement.' Postwar, this was also an era in which the English people's trust in institutions could still be readily exploited. Nowadays reports of abuse in Catholic schools, youth groups, football academies and by celebrities is so widespread that the English harbour residual suspicion towards priests and scout leaders, asking why people would *want* to undertake such roles – what do they really want from such a role? I'll examine shortly the comedians who reconfigured ideas of masculinity, but the idea of positive male role models has been severely undermined by the failure of institutions to put victims before their own reputation, for obtuse fear of damaging the latter. By allowing abuse to take place in such institutions so long the English (and it is clearly *not* just an English issue) placed the vulnerable in a toxic doublebind. By ordering them to trust institutions that abused them. The outcome was then that abused people had to carry on living in a secular world in which the ancient traditions of religion and institutional trust no longer fitted the challenges of their day-to-day reality. People might step outside these institutions and find refuge in pop, but that too was rife with exploiters. In this instance alienation would be a personal, pervasive sense, embedded by ongoing injustice. One of the most galling aspects of the Savile case is that he was never called to account, making one look instead for karmic or religious responsibility. The only possible cold comfort one can glean is that Savile himself was clearly so damaged, and *isn't virtue its own reward*? But the lack of faith the populace have in investigations and enquiries, following the Savile case and the likes of Hillsborough, show that the distrust runs deep. Having kept a vague eye on the ongoing Child Abuse Investigation it has been notable how often investigations into the likes of the late Labour MP Greville Janner, himself accused of multiple child abuse, have been kicked into the long grass to such an extent that the head of the enquiry, Sir Richard Henriques, concluded that 'the primary cause of failing to prosecute Janner in 1991 was, in my judgment, an inefficient investigation by police'. Janner's family continue to protest his innocence, and there have too been proven instances of false accusations. So how are we to get to the bottom of any victim's trauma and resolve it?

In recent years the lustre of celebrity has worn off a little, but without an understanding of how Savile eluded justice the English faith in institutions, the famous and the freedoms of the pop world remain tainted. Whilst institutions and political parties will always prioritise the protection of their own name over the safety of those under their wing, abusers will remain free to exploit our shared sense of institutional boundary for their own means.

Chapter 9

Under the Fridge – from Stephen Fry to Caroline Aherne, Johnny Vegas and James Acaster

The 'Beyond the Fringe' ensemble headed by Peter Cook's genius loci was to morph into a new generation. Hugh Laurie and Stephen Fry, in Richard Curtis' *Blackadder*, would go on to lampoon the type of aristocratic Englishness that Evelyn Waugh had bemoaned the death of. One personified by First World War generals like Stephen Fry's Melchett, who weren't even sure which side of the map the English army were supposed to conquer and who couldn't care less as long as luncheon was served on time. Blackadder's contempt for the working-class Baldrick always seemed to have an edge of affection to it in relation to his view of Melchett. But Blackadder's deepest contempt is reserved for Melchett's aide, Captain Darling, with his echoes of Evelyn Waugh's Hooper, as a man who sees obsequiousness to the upper classes as a means to social climbing. Cook himself – with a typically dismissive attitude towards political invective – had poked fun onstage at Harold Macmillan by portraying him bluffly insisting that England still led the world despite overwhelming evidence to the contrary (a sketch which begs the question of when an up-and-coming comedian will similarly maul Boris Johnson). But by the early eighties the focus of comedians had shifted from the Establishment and on to the underclasses it had apparently neglected.

Whether it was in the lampooning of the earnest student in *Citizen Smith*, or in Rik Mayall's pompous anarchist poet Rick the attention shifted from toothlessly mauling the absurdity of English institutions to mocking the absurdities increasingly fostered within the English psyche. Thatcher's underfunding of realms of the country spawned these types of characters, creating a counterculture whose voice was being increasingly invalidated.

Other denizens of The Comic Strip collective, such as French and Saunders, would go on to lampoon the consumerist delirium of the moneyed upper-middle classes in this neo-liberal age. But beneath the ascending zeppelin of new pomposities there was a darker shadow. The comedy stand-up persona (influenced perhaps by the apparent anxiety within the schtick of Tony Hancock and the like) started to look under the rock for inspiration – less behind the fridge and more *under* it. By the time Johnny Vegas started stand-up, personas began to focus around the very real angst and desperation of the individual who'd been badly side-lined by society. Vegas' schtick was that as a fired Butlin's Red Coat and failed potter (who'd believed 'clay was the way') the stage was the place in which the sorely overlooked finally got their turn in the spotlight. Vegas was a brilliant, rich persona invented by Michael Pennington, but 'summoned' might be a better word than 'invented'. As Pennington's autobiography describes, Vegas was borne out of the sexual frustration, bodily self-loathing and disappointment that Pennington – who had once intended to be a priest – felt. Men like Pennington struggled to find their feet in this brave new world and their animus cultivated into personas like Vegas'. It was curiously cathartic and terrifying to see these personas given voice – particularly under the guise of this apparently entertaining thing called 'comedy'.

Footage of Vegas' early gigs show that his persona was an incarnation, a tapping into the darker side of his psyche that Pennington lent his frame to. Some mysterious combination of alcohol and self-loathing on any given night gave Vegas his voice. As his autobiography reveals, Pennington had a delicate grip on the methods used to bring Vegas to the fore. When he did, Vegas would tell the audience everything Pennington felt but would not express. Vegas was sincere because there was nothing for him to fear any more, his failure was absolute. Vegas would voice to attractive women his loathing of their sexiness, his jealousy of their partners, and he would break the performer-audience boundaries in physically expressing this angst knowing that he was protected in his guise as the performer (which would itself cause controversy). Footage of his early gigs recall Mark E Smith's The Fall. Something powerful, dark and uncontainable was being tapped into and played out on the stage and the bond with the audience was predicated on the thrill of the unpredictable, on the sense that something true is being said. Vegas would often pretend, during his performances, to shout at stagehands that 'he knew he was running over' and pretend to be refusing to go offstage when he was in fact still in his allotted time slot. In so many respects we were getting a sense that this performance was taking us off-grid, to the outside, and from time immemorial we have intuited that it is in this nowhere that we will learn something new, and true

In Vegas' performances there were no rock star poses, no comedian-as-sex-god schtick, as the likes of Russell Brand would later deploy. Vegas was a huge influence on the similarly dark Stewart Lee, who would himself experiment with the form, slowing the pace of performances and twisting the traditional call-and-response nature of jokes. Until the audience were bizarrely laughing at slow, laborious recitals of Lee's grandfather's favourite flavours of crisps.

John Shuttleworth – a character created by Graham Fellows – could easily have been a neighbour of Vegas'. Shuttleworth's lack of self-awareness led him to think that his plinky keyboard numbers such as *Pigeons in Flight* would be selected for the Eurovision Song Contest. In this view of England it is an overlooked land, full of overlooked talent which people refuse to admit would by now have been spotted. Caroline Aherne's Mrs Merton, in the mid-nineties, would appropriate the overlooked and acerbic wit of the working-class elderly, whose opinions are tolerated due to societal deference to age and (slowly fading) ideas of generational respect. If Aherne was sharp but not cruel (the accuracy of her observations belying any suspicion of malevolence) then her nuance was at odds with other comedies of the nineties. The popular sitcom *Peep Show* (first aired in 2003) would also target overlooked urban survivors but there was none of Vegas' catharsis in the sheer misery of the characters Mark and Jeremy, with their loveless co-dependency.

The feckless Jeremy is a relic of the counterculture that the likes of Citizen Smith would've been a part of. Protesting at nothing, always looking for a vaguely artistic and bohemian way of life in which the materialist trappings of pop culture would guarantee some endless meal ticket off the back of artistic status (itself a deeply elitist idea which is never examined). *Peep Show*'s Jeremy personified the laziness and lack of responsibility that the hippies were accused of and showed what happened to this mentality if it was left to evolve for a few decades. There is a hint of *Alfie* in Jeremy. Michael Caine's portrayal of Alfie showed a crisis of masculinity (in the words of Michael Bracewell, *Alfie* 'showed the sex-hungry male – Jack The Lad – as an ultimately weak figure, imprisoned within the suffocating locality of his conquests'). *Peep Show* updates it in Jeremy far better than Jude Law's over-lit rehashing. For all of Jeremy's seeming bohemianism (his tenure in various short-lived bands, his appropriation by local cults) Jeremy is imprisoned within the suffocating proximity of various half-baked cultural ideas that he has appropriated. He wants the sexual freedom of *Alfie* and finds amongst the various women he meets (who have been damaged by the temptations of their youth) rich pickings. He wants the financial income and lifestyle of a pop star, and doesn't see why his lack of talent should be any impediment to that as he has heard about pop stars who have managed that. In fact, Jeremy's view of art is deeply cynical – it offers no talent and has no insight to offer, it is just an easy way to get rich and get laid.

In various situations Jeremy taunts Mark for his uncoolness, and he reaps the rewards of his relative coolness by having sex with the various damaged women that enter his orbit. But it is Mark whose income he relies on (despite Jeremy not having a good word to say about his career) and despite that any proximity to Mark's work life is just another opportunity for Jeremy to damage Mark without apology.

Bracewell defined the 1970s male as 'obsessed with the climate of his feelings…searching for his soul in the closed order of his own mind', adding, 'This was a monk-like, if melodramatic, occupation. It was uncompromising, scornful of indulgence and in favour of a lucidity that would lead to the painful lucidity of true feelings.' *Peep Show*'s Jeremy shows the evolvement of this isolated figure. Jeremy has no inner world, and any lucidity is incredibly painful as it reminds him of the poverty of his internal life. By the nineties the male is no longer searching for his soul as he is convinced his own locus of meaning is somewhere outside of himself, in culture (or in his selective appropriation of it). For Jeremy meaning is somewhere in his favourite records, his first raves, his half-forgotten early sexual experiences. Jeremy is not scornful of indulgence, as post-war neo-liberalism has convinced him it is his birth right, as it appeared to be for the well-padded Baby Boomers. Jeremy has seen too many films and been to too many gigs to be content with an office job, but he is too enthralled to postmodern depictions of anti-heroes to focus on gaining any qualifications, to bettering himself. He is not going to sacrifice himself for things as boring as 'mortgages' ('sign and recline' is his adage, when he's offered a contract). He is psychically marooned in his twenties even when he is edging further into his thirties. His relationship dynamics only grow more toxic as his dreams get further away and as his opportunities to examine his own inadequacies more frequent. Unlike Vegas, Jeremy garners no affection. He can appear to women as harmless and fun, as though he 'gets them' – until any evidence of his convictions is required, and then it is up to people like Mark to protect him.

In *Peep Show* there is an odd split between the male identity. The irresponsible get all the rewards (women, benefits, to be cool) and the responsible pay for their leisure and are treated with scorn for being suckers. There is no interpersonal or artistic outlet for Jeremy's rage, as his whole demeanour is based on some vague appropriation of sixties 'Peace and Love' ideals. And so Jeremy flits between various occupational nooks and crannies, and there is perhaps a whiff of sociopathy about the perpetual destruction he leaves in his wake. Anyone who tries to remind Jeremy of it, as Mark often does, is 'a square' as in *Peep Show* the counterculture has various slights and insults it can use to protect itself against self-reflection. In the series drugs are not the path to some inner enlightenment or some opportunity for insight. They are something foisted on the responsible by the irresponsible. Once under the influence the irresponsible act appallingly, forget about it and the responsible are left to clear it up. *Peep Show* is deeply critical of the counterculture.

Within the show the counterculture is not a hotbed of radical ideas, but a cesspool in which sociopaths parasitically feed off the responsible, and Jeremy's lack of character evolvement has its own built-in message. In the very English persona of Vegas his corpulence and immaturity might make him an object of pity but there is something admirable about his unflinching ability to see himself for what he is. But underneath his seemingly free-spirited attitude Jeremy is irredeemably weak and selfish and he throws his benefactor Mark under the bus again and again, whether it is for the cooler Superhans, or for a quick lay.

If *Peep Show* satirises the hollow bohemian ideals of what became of the English counterculture it doesn't have much good to say about orthodox life either. Mark is determined to be a better man but just loathes himself for lacking everything Jeremy has convinced him he needs. Mark's lack of kindness towards himself is reflected in the show's portrayal of the lack of kindness people have for each other, in a manner that now seems very cynical. When pressured into taking part in a Rainbow Rhythms dance class, Mark is determined to 'firmly keep the lid on' whilst pretending it has come off and that he is freely expressing himself. Jeremy, meanwhile, pretends to be crazy, cynically knowing that to a certain type of woman this abandon will look attractive. Mark is stranded in an office job where he cannot claim to be inspired or charismatic and as the series progresses, he gradually becomes more okay with this. His attempts to 'find himself' through the publication of his history book (*Business Secrets of the Pharaohs*) leads to the counterculture ripping him off in the form of a corrupt publisher pretending to be responsible. Mark 'gives' up Jeremy's ideals in favour of the kind of acceptance of domesticity that will see him enjoy instead the English pleasures of historical nostalgia (Mark's deep interest in Stalingrad is a frequent punchline). In *Peep Show* orthodox life offers nothing but sexual and personal alienation, but the alternatives offered by counterculture are way more toxic, and the polarity in Mark and Jeremy's characters reminds us of this duality again and again. The only third path for Mark is through the psychopathic yuppy mentality of his boss Johnson, who flits between being ingratiating and being shamelessly exploitative with the same lack of self-awareness that Jeremy has acquainted the audience with.

For all that *Peep Show* portrayed the shabby options of middle English life in the 2000s there were even darker portrayals of this hinterland that had richer insight at the time. There are echoes of Vegas in David Earl's brilliant character, Brian Gittins – a café shop owner and frustrated comedian who is too angry, too bitter to find success. Gittins often laments in his short videos that his comedy partner, Angelos Epithemiou, is regularly invited on to the comedy show *Shooting Stars* as a regular and that he is not. The short YouTube series in which Gittins and Epithemiou played off each other on such matters was a dark delight, full of rich nuance. The punchline presumably being that Epithemiou (a north-east burger van owner who considers himself a sexual lothario, despite his ever-present Sainsbury's bag) does not himself understand why Vic Reeves and Bob Mortimer keep inviting him back on to Shooting Stars.

So we aren't really sure who is laughing at who in this very English, Laurel and Hardy style dynamic. The slightly sharper Gittins is laughing at Epithemiou, who is in turn presumably being laughed at by Reeves and Mortimer when they keep inviting him on to Shooting Stars. Epithemiou – an invention of Dan Renton Skinner – became a cult star whilst Gittins' peculiar brand of bitterness became a vein of itself in English comedy. This vein of English comedy – in which an unashamed revelling in squalor (itself deeply revealing about the state of the nation) as a source of comedy was apparent in Caroline Aherne's *The Royle Family*, amongst other comedies. The unhygienic, perpetual masturbator, whose shameless self-indulgence is funny because there is something recognisable and – sadly – peculiarly English about it. This vein of comedy, inspired by a peculiarly English lack of self-awareness, would later see itself echoed in the likes of *The Office* and *I'm Alan Partridge*. Gittins' persona would find fame on Ricky Gervais' comedy series *Derek* in the form of the character Kevin. And in 2020 there were echoes perhaps of Lee, Vegas, and even Shuttleworth in the likes of (self-described) failed musician James Acaster, who turned to comedy after his band (The Wow Scenario) didn't achieve fame.

Acaster's peculiar appeal as a comedian comes from the courageous marshalling of his own personal shame (perhaps the price paid for attention, in his worldview) which first came to light in a series of radio phone-ins to Josh Widdecombe's XFM show. These phone-ins would later be styled as 'James Acaster's Classic Scrapes'. It was an item that featured the idiosyncratically voiced Acaster recalling real-life humiliating episodes (such as the time he missed a last train from Basingstoke and ended up sleeping in a bush in a woman's dress) for the generous pleasure of his listeners. Acaster's persona seems to veer in and out of self-awareness whilst belying a sense of complete control over these manoeuvres. In some respects he plays the classic fool, brought in to amuse the king of the court. But his position as someone who fervently believes they are unfairly overlooked ensures the appreciation of the public, as it is a character the English are used to having in their midst.

Chapter 10

The Moors and Man About the House – Morrissey's Psychogeographic England

On the subject of people believing they are unfairly unlooked – following a terminal adolescence, during the mid-eighties Morrissey revealed himself to be a skilled bricoleur. He chose certain onstage props to associate himself with the disenfranchised, wearing NHS specs and hearing aids to express an emotional kinship with the early-fifties singer Johnny Ray. Gladioli were appropriated in his onstage persona both to reject the sterile, post-industrial atmosphere of 1980s 'super clubs' like Manchester's Hacienda but also, in lieu of lilium, to express a sense of kinship with Oscar Wilde, who decorated his home with flowers at his most persecuted. Their kinship was not just spiritual, however. Both were of Irish descent but came to be regarded as ironic and very English. Morrissey also appropriated a few select cultural influences as part of his oeuvre – from Billy Fury, the *Carry On* films and sit-coms such as *Man About The House*. He cast himself amongst these textscapes, soundscapes and landscapes as an outsider in our midst. But filtered through these texts was also a marshalled pride in being an outsider, a sense that in fact the world could benefit much from those it had long dismissed. One of Morrissey's favourite authors was Radclyffe Hall, and her best-known novel, *The Well Of Loneliness*, depicts the life of a masculine lesbian (who happens to share Morrissey's Christian name, albeit with a different spelling). The working model of reassurance that Morrissey would offer to his fans is beautifully crystallised in the book. Hall wrote:

You're neither unnatural, nor abominable, nor mad; you're as much part of what people call nature as anyone else...

don't shrink from yourself, but just face yourself calmly and bravely. Have courage...show the world that people like you can be quite as selfless and fine as the rest of mankind. Let your life go to prove this – it really would be a great life-work, Stephen.

From his work with The Smiths through to his solo career, Morrissey's engagement with England as a subject matter has been often controversial. In the second track Morrissey and Johnny Marr wrote together for The Smiths, *Suffer Little Children* (which ended up on their debut album) Morrissey appropriated the landscape of the Moors, telling the story of Ian Brady and Myra Hindley's murdered victims. 'I happened to live on the streets where, close by, some of the victims had been picked up,' Morrissey told *The Face* magazine. Figuratively penetrating the veneer of the landscape, he sang 'Over the moor / take me to the moor / dig a shallow grave and then lay me down'. His appropriation of this English terrain took on a psychogeographic quality when he sang of 'fresh lilac moorland fields' which, despite their fragrant exterior, conceal buried truths, and 'cannot hide the stolid stench of death'. Even early in his career, Morrissey's eye is on what he thinks is really going on in our green and sometimes unpleasant land. It is clear too that he is not slow to apportion blame. 'Manchester / So much to answer for', he laments.

By the time he co-wrote the opening track to *The Queen Is Dead* (often considered by fans as The Smiths' masterpiece) he was 'checking registered historical facts' to unearth his own history, and was 'shocked and ashamed to discover / that I'm the 18th pale descendent / of some old queen or other'. His ambiguous use of the word 'queen', with all its homosexual as well as royalist implications, is teasingly Wildean. With the sampling of Florrie Forde's *Dear Old Blighty*, a listener could be excused for thinking Morrissey is expressing affection for this country with the track. But it is an affection that's very much on his own terms, within the constellation of cultural points that he chooses to recognise. He dreams of a Republican England, with 'her very lowness with her head in a sling'. His recollection of schooldays in *The Headmaster's Ritual* (from *Strangeways Here We Come*) seems a long way from *Just William's* summertime japes. 'Belligerent ghouls run Manchester schools,' he intones, addressing teachers he considered 'spineless swines' in possession of 'cemented minds'. Evoking the institutional abuse that would run alongside the nation's gradual erosion of faith in authority he describes how a teacher 'does the military two-step down the nape of my neck'.

Elsewhere, Morrissey's lyrics were harder to read. In his solo track *Bengali in Platforms* (from *Viva Hate)* he urges the Bengali of the title to 'shelve your Western plans' adding 'it's hard enough when you belong here'. Given Morrissey's insistence that there 'was no hatred' in the songs, the kind observer might conclude that, along with *The National Front Disco* (from *Your Arsenal*, 1992) and *Asian Rut* (from *Kill Uncle*, 1991) Morrissey was portraying an England coming to terms with immigration. Certainly, as a lyricist he has a sharp eye for the tensions of his homeland, which he portrays best when drawing from his own reference points. On the track *Now My Heart Is Full*, from *Vauxhall and I*, the listener might wonder if he was talking about his country as a whole when he opened with the lines:

> *There's going to be some trouble*
> *A whole house will need rebuilding*
> *And everyone I love in the house will recline*
> *On an analyst's house quite soon.*

Was he portraying a damaged England, divided between North and South, and rich and poor? Was he saying that his country needs treatment? Appropriating characters from Graham

Greene's *Brighton Rock*, Morrissey sang:

Dallow, Spicer, Pinkie, Cubitt
Every jammy Stretford poet

He thereby cast himself within the company of those select English figures he found relatable. His vision of a country with 'Loafing oafs in all-night chemists' suggested an England he loves enough to cast his weary eye over, if also a country he felt unable to love unconditionally.

On the later track *Maladjusted* he described the sense of unease felt by those trying to fit into a land so in flux. He sang, in throaty declarations that seem to run out of air at the end of each line, of 'semi-perilous lives'. Where he, and presumably another outsider, will:

Jeer the light in the windows
Of all safe and stable homes
Wondering then
What would peace of mind be like.

This is an England in which the outsider has no home, except in the harsh exteriors amongst 'Fulham lights' that 'stretch and invite into the night'. Keeping 'thieves hours', whilst even those ensconced within the homes he passes are no better off. He describes a woman who 'stalks the house / in a low-cut blouse', capturing the anxious sense of a postmodern land waiting for something that will tie it all together. Just as Wilde would be pilloried from within the Establishment, Morrissey too identifies the English tendency to harm our own, with 'stinging bureaucracy' making it 'anything but easy for working girls'. The consequence of all this, he sang, was a 'soulful of loathing'. It might sound bitter, but it also sounds like an England that is only too recognisable.

Morrissey was later criticised for wrapping himself in a Union Jack during a Finsbury Park performance. Morrissey surely was aware of the potency of the flag and yet, as any listener to his music could argue, he remained conflicted about what it resembled. As Tony Parsons would write, for Vox magazine, 'Morrissey sings of England and something black, absurd and hateful at its heart.' This is the case in *Suffer Little Children* as it remains during the time of *Vauxhall and I*.

Morrissey's ambiguity can perhaps be explained by his Irish roots. By the time of his 2004 single *Irish Blood, English Heart* Morrissey would be proudly defining himself as of dual stock. It is as if England has repelled him. He is 'dreaming of a time when the English / Are sick to death of Labour, and Tories / And spit upon the name Oliver Cromwell'. If Morrissey's more recent political observations have justifiably seen opprobrium heaped upon him – for the crime of dangerous ambiguity if nothing else – then one side effect has been that the nuances of his lyrics have seemed of less relevance. But to the fans who have associated themselves with his outsider status, it is fuel to the fire of those who see themselves as unfairly maligned.

Chapter 11

Victoriana, Candlesticks and Mist – The Cure and the Art of Negation

If Morrissey's sense of being denied was key to his work, then the Goth movement also made an art form out of negation. The movement was striking for its use of the negation both in visual landscapes and in soundscapes. Clarity was negated in videos, with the onlooker's gaze often obscured by mist or dry ice. Gothic videos were generally set – like Gothic films – in scenes where the sun was absent, with candles perhaps as the only illumination. Siouxsie and the Banshee's *Face To Face* (1991) sees Siouxsie masked by a gold hood, in a dim-lit, crumbling house with cobwebbed staircases. Perhaps, pop has always been about the seductive art of revealing – both what is inside and outside.

As Charles Mueller wrote, in reference to The Cure's records, 'The fragmented nature of the imagery helps relay a Gothic sense of disintegration.' One of The Cure's most famous records was titled *Disintegration*, with the band's singer, Robert Smith, portrayed amongst a backdrop of shadowed, wilting and decaying vegetation on the cover. In fitting with goths' preoccupation for Victoriana this cover fitted comfortably within the aesthetic palette of crumbling castles, mist and ever-present darkness – all visual cues associated with this movement.

Mueller writes that out of their entire oeuvre, the opening track of The Cure's album *Pornography, One Hundred Years* 'resonated the strongest with goth fans'. *One Hundred Years* is a nihilistic track, which gets round to negating the importance living in its very first line. In it, with his idiosyncratic blend of the gulp and the wail, Smith sings, 'It doesn't matter if we all die.' The negation continues within the arrangement, with a composition built around a repeated, staccato drum riff that stays steady throughout, even as a swarm of guitars build towards the song's climax. Smith begs his way through a lyric sheet in which he implores an undisclosed person to 'meet my mother' before 'the fear takes hold'. The negation of the lyrics is aided by the negation also inherent in the terrain described in the song. A character is described as 'creeping up the stairs in the dark' and as being 'just a piece of new meat / in a clean room'. This character's lack of human quality matches the rawness of the landscape described: a room that evokes the sterile atmosphere of a clinic. In the terrain that is described the warmth and conformity of normal living have been removed. Consistent with Mueller's description of Goth as concerning 'environmental degradation' 'decay' and 'ephemerality' for this song, The Cure created a boundless, emotional rather than physical space, in which Smith's anguish was presented as unresolvable. Just as the song's drum riff does not develop, neither does the lyrical narrative, with Smith describing a state of almost subconscious torment using a wash of lyrical effects wholly consistent with the blurred cover art. Continuous with the unbounded geography of Joy Division's songs the physical space described seems marginal, out of reach of the familiarity and comforts of domesticity. It is hard to draw any conclusions about how connected this deprivation is to any economic backdrop, as the lyrics are fixated on the internal. Any description of physical space seems more akin to a temporary intrusion into the narrator's senses, rather than an evocation of place.

Smith creates a 'living space' for his character, its timeclock the thrum of a repeated drum riff. This living space seems to exist in a layer *under* that which we would consider usual life. An 'innovation at the cultural level' has again taken place, with Smith rearticulating the private space in the way Joy Division rearticulated external, vacant, industrial space.

This combination of the somehow feral, less-than-human character with a stark rhythmic backdrop makes for a powerful, if nightmarish, musical motif. It makes one wonder about the lives of those on the outside and if indeed the backdrop suggests that in some sense 'we are all on the outside', as no other textures are offered within the aural palette.

The humorous, lovable aspect of The Cure would be brought to the fore by Tim Pope's videos of the band. From the cobwebs of *Lullaby* to the feline infested madness of *Lovecats*, the boundless spaces described in Smith's songs would be appropriated by his lipstick-smeared, mad-haired persona as childlike and comfortably creepy rather than as bleak as they would be in *One Hundred Years*. This was an interior emotional world being conveyed, but the backdrop of mansions, cats and mist seemed at times deeply English. Indeed, *Lovecats* recalls the deeply English TS Eliot's poetry book *Old Possum's Book of Practical Cats* and the mischievous character Macavity the Mystery Cat. Smith's uniqueness perhaps was not only in his commitment to his idiosyncratic voice, but in the attachments he fostered to his audience through a catalogue that variously had despair, existential angst and childlike wonder.

But it is too easy to associate all bands of this era with various ruminations on despair, and to draw parallels between their output and the stressed urban environments that they arguably sprang from. But it is worth mentioning that the year after *Disintegration* was released, Liverpool's The La's eponymous album was released. Far from reflecting the urban nature of their surroundings in their music there was a brightness, optimism and stridency in The La's which contrasted strongly with Goth bands of the 1980s. The contrast is often overlooked. Lee Mavers, far from wallowing in urban despair, seemed to find mysticism in the musical legacy of the city and the River Mersey. Record company entanglements and Mavers' perfectionism prevented The La's from following up their debut to firmly establish themselves. But the band would still create a musical bloodline of their own. Bassist John Power would use the final line of The La's album ('the change is cast') to name his own band and create his own body of work. Mavers' confidence seemed to derive not from his place in society, or even from his identity as a Liverpudlian (his devotion to Everton FC perhaps trumping his devotion to his music during his years in obscurity). His confidence instead seemed to come more from his faith in 'the songs'. Footage of Mavers during the band's early music videos shows him stare at the camera with unnerving intensity, his smile suggesting a deep confidence in what he was doing. The La's are too often reductively seen as typical of jangly pop (with the focused use of the open high E string key not only to the application of the term 'jangly' but to other genres like rockabilly). Mavers' late seclusion and the tantalising prospect of their unreleased work all added to the sense of mysticism and frustration around the band. But their blend of optimism and exuberance could have led to the music of the eighties being considered as far more optimistic and forward looking. It was striking that when TV footage showed Margaret Thatcher (whose stringent economic policies arguably added to the sense of deprivation that eighties bands wrote about) being ejected from office it was The La's track *There She Goes* that was the soundtrack on news reports. There was no little irony here: in using this track the sense of excitement in the song seemed to prefigure the optimism of the nineties.

Chapter 12

Pigs, Riots and Taffeta – Brett Anderson's Blakeian Visions

Morrissey's uneasy descriptions of England evolve into something more fractured, even hallucinatory, in the lyrics of Suede's Brett Anderson. The lyrics on Suede's self-titled debut album would stratify new conceptual space within England's cultural life. Brett Anderson portrayed the drug-addled, the sexual outsider, those looking for elation outside the aspirations of normative life. As he sang on an early B-side, 'where the pigs don't fly / I do'.

Suede certainly weren't the only artists to be portraying England during this cultural era. Their rivals Blur would adopt the template for portraying England from The Kinks (with Damon Albarn's debt to Ray Davies evident in Blur's affectionate tribute entitled *Dear Ray* – Davies had given us a point of view through characters called Terry and June in the song *Waterloo Sunset*). But whereas Davies' view of England seemed loving and affectionate, Albarn's characters – from the *Arnold Layne* evoking *Ernold Same* to *Tracy Jacks* (on *Parklife*) appeared sad and lost in neo-liberalism's contemporary manifestations. Not so much 'lazy Sunday afternoons', but more brief bank holidays before it's 'back to work / A.G.A.I.N'.

Albarn would later be widely accused of patronising the working classes in his songs, of glamourising customs and traditions with the insincerity of a tourist. Brett Anderson's vignettes, though, would be darker, and more abstracted, in their view of England. They would also be pretty humourless, though, it has to be said.

The video to Suede's early single *Animal Nitrate* would see the camera's eye hurry from outside a Brutalist tenement, along its bleak walkways and inside a tower block. The interior is revealed as a sleazy performance space. In it, a shiny Taffeta curtain suggests transformation from a bleak urban flat into a liminal space that recalls the pre-war Berlin nightclubs. This is an impression enhanced when drag artists in masks frolic around the band in leopard print. With the band playing amongst figures dressed in pig masks, the allusions to drug-induced conceptual space are clear from the text's landscape. The fact that the camera's eye then retreats from the flat as the song ends implies that it is only within the fleeting boundaries of the pop song – or the drug high – that alternatives to living can be devised. As if that was ever in dispute. The song evokes, as a contrast, the video to Madness' *Our House*, in which the camera entering the house described finds an arguably stereotypical fare in which men in flat caps hammer jauntily on pianos ('and it's usually quite loud', as Suggs helpfully adds).

Bernard Butler's guitar part for the song is a micro-history of contemporary English music in itself. The combination of overdrive and phaser in the opening chords is psychedelic, creating space for Anderson's ideas. The hammered low E string in the verses recall rockabilly, and the slashed B minor and A major chords recall glam rock. The lead guitar of the chorus snatches the melody from BBC police series *Dixon of Dock Green* (making the song a dissection of Englishness, whether consciously or not) whilst showcasing Butler's remarkable technique. He is adept at combining chords with plucked leads in one guitar figure. A trick which itself recalls what Mick Ronson could only do using overdubs during the *Ziggy Stardust* era.

Suede's debut album is full of the temporary conceptual spaces used in the video for *Animal Nitrate*. Lacunae snatched from a culture that won't economically permit something more permanent for the artist who languishes outside orthodox life, in a state of economic uncertainty, a feature of the progressively entrenched dole culture. In *Breakdown*, Anderson sings 'back where the dogs bark / where still life bleeds the concrete white / try not to go too far inside your own mind'. He warns of how becoming a 'king of infinite space', though understandable amongst the mess of concrete that is contemporary England, is not a good route to go down. In *All the Young Dudes* Bowie had asked if the concrete was all around or in his head, and in this song his heir-apparent answers the enquiry. In *The Next Life* the idea of a better alternative is rooted in the deeply mystical Worthing, where Anderson longs to join a lover and 'flog ice-creams / 'til the companies on its knees'. It seems it isn't just concrete that's in his head – England is too. As Anderson explored more deeply in the follow-up album *Dog Man Star,* the English tendency is to long for distant times. In *The Power,* a song unfinished during Butler's tenure with the band, Anderson sings:

> *You might live in a screen kiss*
> *It's a glamorous dream*
> *Or belong to a world that's gone*
> *It's the English disease*

The quote seems just as relevant years later, given the Conservative Party's push towards a Brexit which strives to recapture a bygone Britain, as best personified by Jacob Rees-Mogg. Elsewhere on the album, Anderson's prescient visions of England are of a land locked in revolution. In *We Are the Pigs* he sings:

> *As they call you to the eye of the storm*
> *All the people say 'stay at home tonight'*
> *I say we are the pigs*
> *We are the swine*
> *We are the stars of the firing line*

Just as The Libertines would later sing of 'stylish kids in the riot' who 'set the night on fire' (in *Time For Heroes*), Anderson too foretells of a younger generation rebelling against the orthodoxy. Speaking of the genesis of *Dog Man Star*, Anderson commented, 'I was having visions about songs. Lots of songs were about visions, like *We Are the Pigs*. I was actually having visions of riots in the streets and inventing insane things, living in this surreal world.'

But how insane were these visions? The 2011 London riots that would follow were blamed variously on racial tension, economic decline and financial inequality. All themes Morrissey and Anderson explored in their own lyrics (in his autobiography *Afternoons with The Blinds Drawn*, Anderson would describe Morrissey attending his gigs and covering Suede's *My Insatiable One*, describing his mysterious sense of some baton being passed on). In *We Are the Pigs* Anderson predicts an England increasingly torn apart by drugs and violence, bludgeoned by the heavy shadow of nuclear war-

And as the smack cracks at your window
You wake up with a gun in your mouth
Oh let the nuclear wind blow away my sins
And I'll stay at home in my house

Anderson admits that his own isolation may have fed into this lyrical content – 'I deliberately isolated myself, that was the idea,' he said. 'It was like; I'm going to go up to Highgate and write a fucking album. See you later everyone.'

During the writing of this album, Anderson found his own quintessentially English space. Holed up in Highgate, in his own Haddon Hall, Anderson took up residence in a flat that was, in his words, 'in the basement of this really beautiful, big Gothic place. It had this amazing garden. There was a summer house at the bottom; a real kind of mansion-type vibe.' If the twisted Englishness of the setting was more than conducive to his writing, a surreal quality was added by the proximity of a Mennonite cult living above him. The Mennonites (a sixteenth-century Dutch cult critical of the luxuries of the modern world) would, Anderson states, 'sing hymns all the time'. Their critique of contemporary Britain, as well as their chants, are perhaps apparent in the schoolchildren chanting the outro of We Are the Pigs ('we all watch them burn'). It is a song in which Anderson imagines the future an increasingly divided England is hurtling towards.

Anderson may have been looking ahead, but his mindset was informed by the past. He frequently cites William Blake as an inspiration around this time (and he would evidently be an influence on Suede's later album Night Thoughts, given its choice of title). Anderson gradually immersed himself in the idea of trance-like states as a creative methodology. He claims that much of the imagery on songs like Introducing the Band was a result of him giving his subconscious a free rein. He delved into books on witchcraft, sex and Aleister Crowley, as well as his protégé, Kenneth Anger. Crowley's whole shtick was that, in the practice of 'Magick', the mind can overpower matter. 'It was part of having a fertile imagination,' Anderson states. 'I was quite into all these people that had visions and were slightly off their nut, people like Lewis Carroll.'

This praxis might have reached its zenith by the time Anderson conducted a bizarre interview with the NME. In it, he stated his favourite artist was a creature he'd invented called Jaquoranda. 'I was deadly serious about it,' Anderson states. 'It had a deer's head and wore a sari!'

Chapter 13

The Other Morrissey – Paul Gascoigne, TFI Friday and Ladettes

The Euro 96 football tournament saw England's disparate view of itself start to coalesce, despite its various ongoing uncertainties about its place in the world, post-war. Shared national agency has often been driven by a sense of achievement we glean from our representatives, and the flair and character of the England team during this era had an invigorating effect on the nation. It was the first time since 1966 that an English team seemed in command of considerable talent and cohesion. In turn, the invigorated nation further invigorated the team. There was a shared audacity about the skill that Paul Gascoigne (surely our finest player since 1966) displayed. Passing to players with back-heels in matches against Switzerland, or lobbing players before scoring with a searing volley, as he did against Scotland in Euro 96.

As the tournament began, with England mindful of the spirit of '66 as a host nation, the land was in a state of joyful rebellion against its own dourness. The private male spaces of the pub and the couch became public performative spaces. Baddiel and Skinner's *Fantasy Football League* reclaimed the layout of a living room on match day as a studio setting, inviting the audience in on the private jokes exchanged between friends during a match. In retrospect it was the beginning of the patronising idea that the everyman is an expert, the kind of collective slip up that would spawn the career of Adrian Chiles, a commentator who, as Stewart Lee said, is 'not a know-it-all, but a know-a-bit'. *TFI Friday* exploded the idea of a pub, making it a visual enterprise in which the audience – as Chris Evans held court behind a pint – became part of the action. This was an idea later built upon in the popular cookery shows hosted by Nigella Lawson, where the private impetuous to play a welcoming host, mother and partner would become a public and charismatic spectacle using the hitherto private space of the kitchen, with Lawson adopting Mediterranean ideas of hosting largesse into the classical Englishness of her feminine persona (at once coquettish and maternal).

On TFI Friday the audience would be drawn into in-jokes that became regular features. Items such as 'Freak or Unique' and 'Fat Lookalikes' suggested, in retrospect, a playground bully marshalling weaker personalities in constant pursuit of his own amusement. If no one was quite sure what they were laughing at, the overriding sentiment seemed to be to 'get over yourself and join in'. It was all deeply laddish and subtly subversive, but whilst it was fun no one objected.

By inviting lesser-known indie bands to perform for huge audiences on his show, and in making Jarvis Cocker a household name simply by referring to him as 'Jarvis', Evans became one of the era's tastemakers. In fairness he did also expose the public to bands (from Dark Star to Shed Seven) who might not otherwise have got TV coverage. It was like the school bully had decided that your band was cool, and in so doing had opened up their world. He was Tony Wilson with ginger hair and NHS specs.

Pride in being English, and pride for our football team became less about football and more of a defiant statement of collectiveness. It even became about agency – with the middle classes to perform their sense of earthiness with exuberant support for a team they probably couldn't name a player of. Shouts of 'he's lost a yard up front' and 'man on' from full-time financial investors must have been quite something to hear.

Paul Gascoigne's 'Dentist Chair' celebration after he scored against Scotland in the tournament's group stage typified this development. Just as teammates had sprayed alcohol directly down his throat during a pre-tournament party, Gascoigne conspicuously replayed this private behaviour as a public spectacle after scoring for England – with the sprayed alcohol performed by teammates in the form of a squirted water bottle. We all wanted to be in on the joke, to perform our affiliation with this team. Gascoigne seemed touched – by divine talent if nothing else – and the white heat of the excitement coalesced around his rather childlike brilliance.

The TV show *My Summer with Des* had archetypal nineties lad Neil Morrissey narrate a summer of heartache as he follows the England team through their glorious tournament performance through to the obligatory penalty heartache. Playing the role of a time-jumping muse who refuses to answer questions, Rachel Weisz is his mercurial object of desire. She also arguably personifies the out-of-time quality of Morrissey's elusive sense of satisfaction, standing as proxy for our own. When England beat Spain in a quarter-final penalty shoot-out, Morrissey's character is so excited that he demands that Weisz takes them forward in time, to the semi-final against Germany, which is now a match he can't wait for. 'Would you not rather enjoy this time?' Weisz's nameless character asks, with a tone that betrays that she knows that the dream will end at the semi-final match. Writer Arthur Smith's portrayal of the feminine in Rachel Weisz's character is curious, heavily freighted as it is with the vague aspirations of the era. Culture always idealises what it hasn't yet realised, lending period pieces a curiously doubled nostalgia in retrospect.

In many ways Weisz's character represents the archetypal 'English rose', with her petite cardigans, dark mane and blood red lips. But there is an added layer of psychic mysticism woven in – she is also a poet. 'You're a city boy, Martin,' she says, 'you need the sadness of the streets.' In her insight, her empathy and her maturity she is far more accomplished and interesting than our centre-stage protagonist, who responds to her poeticism with, 'I'd like to see every city in the world. Except Birmingham.' Having been shunted from the limelight by a boy-child it is her ability to down a pint and enjoy the game which Morrissey's character finds devastatingly attractive. In the show there is nothing incongruous about these various character components. For a brief period of time, under the banner of 'ladette', women's identity was being conspicuously renegotiated. *My Summer with Des* shows a curious time in which this identity was morphing, unapologetic in its lack of resolve. But the incompatibilities between the characters are there, waiting to be engaged. When Weisz's character encourages him to take a different perspective on life, he snarls that she is talking 'hippy crap', and their shared bubble bursts.

The show portrays a brief moment in time. When England's baser enthusiasms – for beer, patriotism and football – had coalesced to exert pressure on those who did not buy into them as mean-spirited and dour. Even though Morrissey's character at the start of the show (from the vantage point of 1998) bemoans the contemporary presence of sleaze, Teletubbies and New Labour he does not realise what halcyon days of fleeting hope he is living in. A brief time in which the slovenly behaviour and lack of ambition of the English 'lad' could credibly elicit the affections of a woman as beautiful and layered and interesting as Weisz's character. As England perform on the pitch, their followers perform to each other their identity with a lack of apology that is *almost* charismatic. But – like with pop songs – the football match only exists within narrow boundaries, even with penalty shootouts or extended codas. As exuberant as the supporters are they cannot shape what occurs in the field of play. Their only choice is their investment in each moment, an idea played with in the script. The duration is a conceptual space in which the personal can be conspicuously performed and resolved until the sanctioned time comes to an end.

This was an era in which the likes of Damon Albarn would conspicuously perform their laddishness with sudden support for Chelsea Football Team (pedants would note that given his birthplace, Leyton Orient would've been a more apt choice). Despite a valiant attempt to stretch the performance until the finale the England team fall short, are knocked out by Germany, and new failure becomes part of an older English mythology. The identity that was in flux builds into it glorious failure as a key and, rather enduring, feature. In time, the overarching framework of hope felt by the country would buckle. New Labour would crash amongst the wreckage of broken promises and recriminations about the Iraq War, despite its many achievements – not least its relatively generous funding of schools and health care, in contrast to the Conservative Party's austerity programme. Viewed in retrospect this era seems charming, given its bolshiness and its naivety. But it also seems unnerving given its subtle but precise exclusiveness.

Chapter 14

Feather Boas and Crimplene – Pulp, Romo, Placebo, Velvet Goldmine and PJ Harvey

In the nineties, an era of pop history flashed past in which all manner of detritus from the past was re-engaged. Amongst the vintage instrumentation of Farfisas, Stylophones and Moogs, amongst the charity shop clothes and the lyrical references to cheap fabrics there was, in the music of Pulp, a sense of a lost future being reinvigorated too.

Sheffield is a city that has long been taunted by promises of the future. From books entitled *Sheffield: Emerging City* (1969) to the propaganda film *Sheffield: City On The Move* (2015), its residents have been constantly bombarded with utopian visions of how their city would soon be, with each idea then shelved over lack of money (despite the millions that would be poured into investments in London's Canary Wharf and Boris Johnson's abandoned garden bridge). As Pulp violinist Russell Senior reflected, 'We grew up reading the local paper and seeing "Sheffield, city of the future", with a map of everyone walking around in space-suits, smiling.' Having taken this aspiration to heart, Jarvis Cocker recalls thinking, 'It's alright if I'm signing on because I'll be on Mars soon.' In retrospect it is not just personal but political naivety that could be blamed for these disappointments. Recalling New Labour's workforce schemes, Cocker would later sing, in *Glory Days*, of how, 'We were brought up on the space race / Now they expect us to clean toilets'. When the rocket into the future didn't take off people were left amongst the wreckage of the present and the past. Pulp would turn this prevailing mood into an art form.

Owen Hatherley talks of how 'Pulp's mid-nineties videos and sleeves mined charity shop clothes for their overlooked, esoteric or recherché properties.' The sheer colour, synthetic nature and eclecticism of the objects Pulp used in this era evidenced some very skilful bricoleurs at work. Or was it merely that Pulp had within their ranks some rather rum characters? Jarvis Cocker, in interviews, would bemoan his reluctance to throw anything away. Russell Senior, the violinist, would go on to run an antiques shop in which, one imagines, thrilling and aborted English futures would be fleetingly evident. Even keyboardist Candida Doyle, known within the band for her 'rinky-dink' style of oversized plastic jewellery and cutesy dresses, was operating within her own recherché bubble.

If there is a thread to Pulp's output it is in their appropriation of the discarded and marginalised, and the will to prioritise – even fetishise – them as sexually potent within their work. In *His 'n' Hers* album track *Pink Glove* Cocker appropriates the glove not just as an accessory, but also as a tool of sexual manipulation. Cocker addresses a woman going to visit her lover, and warns her, 'He doesn't care what it looks like / Just as long as its pink and its tight'. Carnal allusions aside, he details the power play afoot. Cocker warns, 'he's got your heart / he's got control / you might as well know'.

It is as if in focusing on the erotic potential of synthetic materials from bygone eras Cocker was trying to experience, for himself and the listener, the lost potential of these objects (and by extension, the past). In so doing he evokes memories of Walter Benjamin's aborted *Arcades Project*, which attempted to unearth within the contents of the Parisian arcade impulses that had been overlooked and dissolved. In *Myth and Metropolis* Graeme Gilloch chronicles Benjamin's analysis of the modern metropolis, arguing that 'for Benjamin, the edifices and the objects of the metropolis are utopian wish-images, frozen representations or objectifications of genuine wants and aspirations that remain unfulfilled or thwarted'.

As tacky and kitsch as the décor in Pulp videos was, it

was seemingly used as part of a push towards a lifestyle that was unrealised (hence the objects' marginalisation). Pulp's appropriation of overlooked objects – and arguably people – in their music is all part of an artistic will to foreground the background. In so doing, they mine the charity shops, jumble sales and clearing lines of England's past, in an invigorating attempt to suggest alternative futures. Pulp's eventual critical and commercial success then renders this act a thrilling spectacle and an inspiration for the *Freaks* they addressed on their second album. There is also a curious timelessness to Pulp's work, given their conscious attempts to innovate a sense of 'now' within their output.

Pulp's manifesto – whatever it might be – was hinted at in their sleeve messages from 1993 onwards. In capital letters, communiqués to the listener were issued. They variously concerned the fear of soft furnishings, the smugness of coupledom and the need for the outsider to assert themselves. 'We just want the right to be different. That's all,' declared the sleeve of 1997's *Different Class*. Distancing themselves from the amateurish record sleeves of their earlier work on Fire records, Pulp's sleeves were now skilful combinations of high glamour that looked artfully dated on arrival – itself a witty and ironic praxis. The Designers Republic created ostentatiously posed sans serif frame paintings by Phillip Castle, which preserved the group in a manner that suggested that the group's work had gained clarity, definition and objectivity.

The B-side to their single *Lipgloss, Deep Fried in Kelvin* preconfigures the kind of rebellious voice Pulp would perfect in tracks like *I-Spy* ('Can't you see a giant walks looking through your petty lives?') and most sharply in their number two single *Common People* ('you will never understand how it feels to live your life / with no meaning or control'). After a long instrumental, *Kelvin* contains a menacing spoken-word narration in which Cocker intones, 'we don't need your sad attempts at social conscience based on taxi rides home from exhibition openings'. Echoing the subject matter of Morrissey and Marr's second song, he adds, 'Suffer the little children to come unto me / And I will feed them fizzy orange and chips / That they may grow up straight and tall / To live on Kelvin'. Here, Cocker's outsider voice seems to appropriate those so affected by their urban environment that they too have become brutalised in their worldview.

These cutting observations were now married to a synthetic, glossy form of instrumentation, ensuring they were finally ensnaring the interests of large audiences. Elsewhere in the song, the depiction of a man depositing a large quantity of soil in his tower block because 'all he wanted was a garden' portrays the convulsed dreams of the urbanite cut off from the comforts of a rural past that they now craved. In fact, the tight production evokes a sense of urban claustrophobia throughout, of consciousnesses warped by the nature of their existence. The economic realities of the age were being confidentially depicted at last. Once they had finally connected with the masses some subversion was sure to occur.

Given their articulacy, it is a shame some of Pulp's most cutting tracks were delegated to B-sides. Such was the subtly bullying nature of the New Labour movement, which marked any opposition as racist or Tory, Pulp did not feel able to release the sarcastic *Cocaine Socialism* as a single. As a song, it depicted the unease which artists of this era felt following attempts by the Blair government to recruit them. It opened with the words:

I thought that you were joking
When you said you want to see me
To discuss our contribution
To the future of our nation's heart and soul
Six o' clock, my place
Whitehall

The grinning insincerity of everyman Tony Blair is sharply portrayed in the lines, 'I'd just like to tell you / that I love all of your albums'. Cocker has a dig at the insincerity of the ruling elite, with the lines 'can you sign this for my daughter / she's in hospital / her name is Miriam?' being followed by 'do you want a line of this?' (Incidentally, this piece does not pretend to accuse Blair of cocaine use. His alleged crimes are well documented and beyond the remit of this (or, in fairness most) volumes.)

In the song the politician depicted pleads for the singer's support, saying, 'we've waited such a long time / for the chance to help our own kind', deftly adding the self-interest that undercut apparent socialism with the words, 'you owe it to yourself / don't think of anybody else'. Having asked 'are you a socialist?' the song concludes with the line 'we promise we won't tell'. The implications are clear – a political party coercing others under the banner of socialism was in fact really interested in enriching its own. A conclusion which seems inescapable following Blair's rabid, insistent and baffling pursuit of enormous wealth in the service of foreign dictators, after leaving office. Cocker was not just a sharp social observer, but a prescient one.

Regardless, this was an era in which the past was seen as *now*. The mid-nineties Romo scene, based around Club Skinny in Camden, would see musicians indebted to New Romantics party, acting as if the Blitz Club had never closed, whilst asserting the contemporary nature of their practice when questioned. The spark illuminating this scene was the sheer textual, almost erotic thrill of the synthetic. Romo was a cult that was all surface, no feeling. Amongst the landfill shoegazing acts in thrall to some vague ideas of authenticity at the time the shameless revitalisation of the idea that the surface was all was thrilling. Their key argument was that they were, according to Simon Price, 'a violent reaction against nostalgia'; they were Futurist. But the shakiness of the record deals offered and the lack of comradeship between bands like Sexus and DexDexter meant that such cosmetic preoccupations did not help matters, and there was to be no hit Romo record (even if their aesthetic is arguably apparent in acts like La Roux). Orlando were the only Romo band to actually release an album, and the aloofness that characterised Romo was, in the words of their vocalist Dickon Edwards, part of the scene's inbuilt obsolescence. 'It was a weird lonely scene,' he said. 'The scene lesson is to be nice to everyone, rather than standoffish and aloof.' Herein is surely the intrinsic problem with these scenes. Without some sort of inclusion criteria their potency is lost, but a sense of snootiness hardly encourages the kind of inclusion that an organic development of it would require. The DNA of Romo would be continued in the glam-rock night Stay Beautiful, which appropriated a Velvet Goldmine of glamour including the early Manic Street Preachers, early Placebo and which looked to Ziggy Stardust era Bowie and Iggy Pop as scene elders.

The 1998 Todd Haynes cult film *Velvet Goldmine* tells the story of David Bowie and Iggy Pop through every visual and aural cue possible, deploying textscapes, landscapes and soundscapes to their maximum capacity for the knowing, whilst skirting any actual mentions of them out of legal necessity (David Bowie had refused to offer the rights to his work for use in the film).

In its exuberant and lovable portrayal of the rise and fall of glam-rock star Brian Slade (whose name evokes the glitter-rockers Slade) the film exerts its 'newness' with appearances from members of contemporary bands such as Suede, Radiohead and Placebo, whilst languishing in the visual cues of glam rock, such as we might have visualised them in the nineties. The film's appeal, for all its flaws, lies in the way it sharpens the audience's focus on all they love about Ziggy Stardust era glam rock. The spandex, the androgyny, the mock-Edwardian dress, all slathered in plenty of sequins and glitter. There was a precedent to the imperative to take dress from another era and glamourise it, given Adam Ant had appropriated the persona of that English fugitive figure – the highwayman – to commercial effect. This all allowed the film to feel familiar, and yet it is bright and exuberant enough to also feel fresh. The film promises 'a land where all things are perfect and poisonous', and it is tempting to map that conceptual space as being spiritually habituated by the group of artists – from Brian Eno to Lindsay Kemp – who offered the soundscapes of the film.

The contemporary artists featured in the film in this era also seemed to be reclaiming their cultural past whilst redefining exactly what it was. In their own output Placebo would express private teenage and existential pain over glam-rock guitars, whilst embracing the practical uncertainties of camp in their lyrics. Although they were a pretty new band at this point, they were indebted to the past, and when they shed the glam-rock sound on their third album to embrace hip-hop and electronica they seemed to falter – before they composed themselves again on the album *Sleeping With Ghosts*. The mood of songs such as *Teenage Angst* and *Pure Morning* would portray the exhaustion that followed the implied sexual decadence described in their songs. In the final two tracks of their debut album, the Jean Genet inspired *Lady of the Flowers* and the album closer *Swallow* would in fact capture a liminal mood evocative of extreme drug-fuelled or post-coital states with a sensitive sensuality.

But it wasn't just their soundscapes that achieved this. Using evocative sleeves that portrayed skinny, under-dressed and dazed figures gripping each other in emptied, Ballardian swimming pools and overgrown trailer parks, their landscapes served to enhance this effect too. The photography of Corrinne Day, who became known for her photographs of Kate Moss, was commissioned in Placebo's most sharply conceptualised period. The shaded seventies interiors, ruined patios, overgrown gardens and algae-filled swimming pools of Day's fashion photographs for i-D, Vogue and Face magazine reflected, embodied and landscaped the soundscapes and textscapes of Placebo's work to under-appreciated effect.

Around this time the Dorset-born artist PJ Harvey adopted a more glam-rock aesthetic too. Emerging with her debut album *Dry* – a witty, desperate blend of blues and rock – her image had been that of an off-duty ballerina – severe and unadorned. By the time of her single *50 Ft Queenie* and its attending album *Rid Of Me,* leopard print and kitsch sunglasses had been thrown into the mix. Harvey's third album, *To Bring You My Love,* was concerned with a swampier take on the blues, and aurally evoked claustrophobic interiors related to lovelorn emotional states. In an opposing way (perhaps smothering the rawness of her expression with cosmetics) Harvey performed its tracks at that year's Glastonbury in a skin-tight pink cat suit, high heels, wearing lurid blue eye shadow with false eyelashes. It was a look she would dub 'Joan Crawford on acid' and when explaining her appropriations it was clear they were chosen to distance herself as a person from the personal nature of the songs. In the time-honoured fashion, Harvey was wearing a mask to tell the truth.

In her later albums, Harvey would use female characters to reveal the pain of her inner world against an increasingly English backdrop. On the sorely underrated *Is This Desire?* a prostitute named Angelene is 'the prettiest mess you've ever seen', whose dreams of going 'a thousand miles away' are expressed with a palpable ache by Harvey's voice. On this album Harvey utilises her breathing to innovative and moving effect, starting lines with insufficient breath so that by their end there is a sense of the singer having been hollowed out by her experiences.

The song *The Wind* is inspired by Saint Catherine and the Saint Catherine's Chapel in Abbotsbury. As Kate Bush's Catherine had haunted Heathcliff on a remote English hill, this song links to it by pinning another Catherine to a chapel on a hill. It inverts a traditional prayer women there used to pray for a husband in its lyrics. *Is This Desire?* is an album that deploys various English locations as fertile ground for extreme emotional states, from the chapel in *The Wind* to the bleak seaside hotel used in the video for *A Perfect Day Elise.* In this track a claustrophobic breakup is visually portrayed with nuances that will emotionally snag those familiar with such places. What Harvey was revealing through these mouthpieces remains speculative, but the emotional impact of the songs is indisputable. Bush and Harvey both appropriated English sites – the bleak hillside, the forgotten seaside hotel – as backdrops for their own depictions of liminal emotional states.

Soon after Harvey would sing on the Tricky track *Broken Homes* (off his 1998 album *Angels with Dirty Faces*), her voice that of a female commentator warning someone of how 'those men will break your bones' and how they 'don't know how to build stable homes'. As a child of broken homes himself, Tricky, AKA Adrian Thaws, would blend exotic rhythms and electronica on tracks like *Ponderosa,* the lyrics of which would subvert the bucolic image of the English weeping willow to portray a more contemporary reality. 'Underneath the weeping willow,' he growled, 'lies a weeping wino.' Tricky would also blend genders with his use of female dress in a manner that recalled David Bowie on the cover of *The Man Who Sold the World,* therefore personifying in his appearance contemporary England with its blend of race and gender.

On PJ Harvey's album *Let England Shake,* the mouthpieces and masks would start to be removed. Harvey would come across as a more objective narrator of England's troubles, no longer using the country as a backdrop but instead making it the subject matter. 'The West's asleep,' she sang, 'Let England shake.' In an album which seemed haunted by the bugles of England's past wars, Harvey summed up her conclusion – 'England's dancing days are gone,' she sang.

Chapter 15

Ghosts, Hauntings and Mezzanines – Massive Attack, Tricky, Dizzee Rascal and Stormzy

Tricky warrants far more than a brief mention, seeing that he emerged from a hugely influential scene that was richly influential to the English perception of itself. The Bristol Massive Attack collective combined graffiti artists, rappers and DJs, and evoked the kind of commune-dwelling artsy collectives of the 1980s. Not least in that their true coalescence – if Tricky's autobiography is to believed – belatedly occurred around a major record deal. It was a deal that would soon lead to their highly influential debut, *Blue Lines*.

What is striking about *Blue Lines*, even decades on, is its sheer freshness. Particularly given the intrinsically derivative nature of the sampling that formed its musical core. It was an album which gave mainstream voice to various, less exposed figures on the British scene. Culture was being cut and pasted through the use of aural samples, but the vocals laid on top of them were allowing for deep self-expression to take place as the top layer of the tracks. Horace Andy was a Jamaican roots reggae singer, and his rich, soulful voice on *The Big Wheel* not only added even more range to this eclectic album but also leant its finale a kind of philosophical weight, with its references to the cyclical nature of experience. Shara Nelson (who co-wrote and produced four tracks on the album, and whose influence is often underrated) contributed soaring vocals on the hit *Unfinished Symphony*, a song that would be remarkable for many reasons, not least its distinctive production. The track used a real orchestra amongst all the samples, a juxtaposition which had been rarely seen in hip-hop. It also, in the words of DJ Mushroom, made the song 'heavier and deeper with more feeling'. This was an album –

and a collective – which produced a startling and subtle range of textures – from the mellow groove of *Daydreaming* to the verbosity of *Five Man Army* (with its witty mentions of Subbuteo and Visa Cards). The album also was the launch pad for new voices. Tricky, who would become an unusually artistic presence on the music scene, is just one example. He began to leave the shadow of Massive Attack, having started to find his voice on *Blue Lines* tracks like *Five Man Army*. But the self-effacing, angry growl he became most famous for would come later.

On his debut album *Maxinquaye*, it was as if the sheer stifled anger Tricky had about his life was framed in his vocal delivery style – submerged as it was beneath the dub bass, never pushed to the fore live. Tricky seemed less interested in fame than in simply living his life, and it became evident he would only release his work if he could do it his way. There would be no compromising. From this era only PJ Harvey seemed to maintain such a stoic sense of loyalty to the moral and artistic judgements made by the creative subconscious whilst being a highly commercial musician.

If Tricky wanted to wear a dress he did, and his lyrics were often vocalised by women such as Alison Goldfrapp and Martina Topley-Bird. Tricky 'othered' himself, not only in that he did not seem to firmly represent his own identity (young, male and black) but also in that it was rarely him serving as figurehead for the 'Tricky' brand. Live, he stepped back from the mike, letting female leads offer the main vocal, seizing their mike when the impetuous took him and often turning away from it, being far from it. In his words he 'like[d] putting women in a male role, to have the woman play the strength and the man be the weak' (presumably through him often being the auxiliary vocalist). It all enhanced the sense that gender and sexuality were part of a fluid spectrum even within this musical milieu. Given the context this was truly ground-breaking. Tricky was 'othered' also in that he did not heed expectations that come with a vocalist performing under their moniker onstage. Live performances of tracks like *Vent* (from *Pre-Millennium Tension*, 1996) would use a single line from the song and repeat it to trance-like effect. Everything became *Aftermath*; connective, representative of the transitory, the in-transmission. In this determined otherness there was a shamanic quality, not least in the aggregate effect of all this othering. Mark Fisher accurately identified the uncanny quality of Tricky. In his words, given 'the women that sing for him / as him, Tricky becomes less than one, a split subject that can never be restored to wholeness'. Perhaps in so doing Tricky captured the fragmented identities prevalent in postmodern living, the different 'hats' people are required to seamlessly transition between in order to navigate their life. Through this fragmentation Tricky was also reflecting the permanent disarray in *Broken Homes* which would never be resolved – either practically or in a psychoanalytic sense.

Fisher proposed that his 'incompleteness [made Tricky] more than one' – a multiplicity, a collective of voices that we might associate with ideas of multiple selves forming a spiritual, unitary identity. Fisher noted too the unusual nuanced textures of Tricky's vocalists, saying, 'What the voices of his female singers – flat, drained, destitute of ordinary affective cadences – most resemble is the sound of a medium, a voice being spoken by something else.' As Martina Topley-Bird sang on *I Be The Prophet*, 'I am already on the other side.' Tricky would speculate in interviews as to where striking lines (particularly 'your eyes resemble mine') would come from in his work. He said, 'I never understand why I write as a female; I think I've got my mum's talent, I'm her vehicle. So I need a woman to sing that.' His mother would lend his debut album its name, as well as its voice. Tricky was haunted by his mother and the departed and yet powerful female voices he associated with more than any absent males. In his words, 'I didn't see my dad, I was brought up by grandmother and auntie...they fed me, clothed me, taught me to steal.' He was also, in a sense, offering a haunting through his samples (the ghostly quality of the vinyl crackle on *Maxinquaye*). As Fisher said, 'writers have to tune into other voices; performers must be able to be taken over by other forces', and he talked of Tricky's 'head-shaking self-erasure'. I agree that this is a prerequisite of the serious artist but – PJ Harvey and perhaps Brett Anderson aside – there were few commercial artists undertaking this praxis during that era. Tricky is not the voice calling out to future destinations, but merely the ghostly hand on the tiller. His first single, *Aftermath*, sampled Japan's song *Ghosts*. Given how much Tricky's album would be concerned with ghosts of influential figures in his life, it was a fitting choice. As Ian Penman would write of his debut album, 'Tricky sounds like ghosts from another solar system.' He acts as shaman for the ghosts trailing out streets, stranded in unresolved states of anguish and identity crisis.

What was initially so interesting about the 'trip-hop' scene that Tricky was lumped in with was its lack of a declarative quality, which conversely meant that something much more interesting was going on than was perhaps appreciated. The braggadocio that some readily associated with rap was in no way apparent. Tricky's marijuana induced introspection was so distinct as to carry into his work a consciousness that was unique. This may have been a symptom of him never feeling he belonged in any camp. In his words, friends in the ethnic ghetto would say, 'why do you hang out with those skinhead guys, the white guys?' He would always have a foot in both worlds, which was reflected not only in aspects of his music – such as the dub bass and the post-punk positioning of vocals behind the usual rock ensemble, but also in his sensibility. The spectral quality hinted at in Penman's consideration is there in 'the way it refused to step up or represent, the way it slurred between lucidity and articulacy'. It was not just liminal in its representation of English landscapes (the stoners flat, the sealed off urban zone accessible only through withdrawal and lawlessness, the penthouse of the rich and famous); it was liminal within its own form. With *Aftermath*'s sampling of the film *Bladerunner* it was alien in soundscape as well as sensibility.

But what to me is most striking about Tricky's voice on his solo albums is how much it captures that of the seething, overlooked man, one kept on the fringes of society. The Specials, whose ska music often concerned urban disintegration on the likes of *Ghost Town*, had always retained something of a jauntiness which was wholly absent here. Tricky's voice, deepened by weed, itself evokes the tenements and mezzanines that Massive Attack would later turn their attention to on the likes of their later, 1998 album *Mezzanine*. On *Mezzanine* we are placed in a lyrical landscape of building firms (Group Four) tearing down and rebuilding our outer and therefore inner world, in which 'relay cameras monitor / and the buzz surrounds'. On this track our multi-voiced protagonist tries to harden themselves against the toughness of suburban life, rapping about how they 'train[s myself] in martial arts'. In the subterranean symphony that is the title track, a fraught world is portrayed in which our narrator is tense about 'crowded scenes', where 'traffic grows' and 'windows hum'. Elsewhere, *Inertia Creeps*.

Massive Attack depicted a world of alarms, of unexpressed frustration, tenseness and fear. The push for commercial efficiency in a neo-liberal society has led to a fragmentation in identity that is unresolved, but the individual is responsible for that state. The fact that Massive Attack's canvas was broad enough to incorporate the likes of Elizabeth Fraser, on the track *Teardrop*, showed the vast range of their output. Fraser (best known for singing in a childlike, made-up language in her band The Cocteau Twins) might not have seemed an obvious choice for such an urban album – but the choice was inspired. A voice which had for long seemed to channel the divine worked as a striking note of clarity on an album which built such a concrete inspired miasma. In fact, the choice of Fraser almost suggests the presence of the divine amongst the humdrum – as if reminding us that in this realm of broken identities the divine serves its function.

Goldie, hailing from a background of drum 'n' bass, had found fame with a song about *Inner City Pressure* and in his later work, like the single *Temper Temper*, we could also hear the juxtaposition of anger and urban pressure. We can see the influence of Massive Attack, arguably, on later work by rappers like Dizzee Rascal not only in their breadth (Dizzee's work was eclectic enough to cover garage, hip-hop and R&B) but in the lyrical subject matter too. He, too, is a *Boy in da Corner*, articulating his overlooked status with enough energy to make himself the UK's first internationally recognised rap star, prising the vibrant grime scene into the mass consciousness in the process. Dizzee was not embarrassed by his presence, or in any way haunted. Where Massive Attack often used a more understated style, Dizzee was fluid, articulate, verbose – his lyrics a dazzling array of images and articulations. He seized his identity as a young black male and in doing so with confidence made the overlooked individual centre stage. We could later see evidence of his barnstorming in the way that Stormzy built on his breakthrough. In Stormzy's 2019 headlining Glastonbury set there was the exhilarating sense that all these vibrant scenes were finally being acknowledged for their over-ground status, not least when he paid heartfelt tribute to the likes of Dizzee, Chipmunk and Kano. There was the sense too that these collectives had collected and harnessed the power of their individual members to create something powerful enough to address the mass consciousness.

Chapter 16

Dickensian Pop and Arcady – The Libertines, Queen Boadicea, Patrick Wolf and Billy Childish

A sense of romance can be fostered by mere inaccessibility. The romantic vision members of The Libertines had of London in their youth was fostered by it having been so out of reach for them. Being from Northumberland and Hampshire respectively, Peter Doherty and Carl Barât pined for the capital. In his autobiography Barât describes his romantic dreams of London being concerned with its 'decaying beauty and brittle, tawdry sheen of glamour'. Before the constellation of influences that would coalesce into The Libertines were formed, Peter Doherty would move to the capital, nurturing his own ambitions for it. In his own words he was soon 'getting a lot from London'. As an aspiring poet constantly teetering between aspiration and pretension, he would wander 'the wards', an ancient term for the boroughs of London, and marvel how 'just three or four streets would contain its own dialect, culture, even [their] own flag'. In the early days of his artistic partnership, he and Carl Barât would 'wander the wards' together. It isn't hard to imagine how a partnership in thrall of a dialectical England, mindful of its capacity to drape itself in localised flags, would soon adopt the red colonial jackets worn by Michael Caine in *Zulu* as part of their onstage attire. The pair stole the jackets from vintage stores in Camden, adding a layer of lawlessness to their shared sense of wanderlust – one which would soon overpower their fragile partnership. A partnership that first deepened when Doherty started to put on what he called 'Arcadian Cabaret Nights' at the Foundry on Old Street.

In the early days of The Libertines, Barât and Doherty developed a shared mythology group; one in which their partnership was steering 'The good ship Albion' (a metaphor for Britain) to the paradise of Arcadia. We can only wonder how these dreams of a distant Albion would have been interpreted by youth subculture post Brexit. To Doherty's mind, Arcadia was 'the realm of the infinity...not a cult or a religion...but an awareness of your surroundings'. In interviews he would talk of it as a quasi-mystical glade, which a wandering minstrel such as he could stumble upon, and in so doing, enter a utopian place. Rhian Jones summarised the Libertine's impulse towards the utopian as an attempt to 'transplant Merrie England's agrarian communism to a mock-Dickensian urban utopia – where it functions as an ideal to be attained collectively, perhaps, but by substance-fuelled escape into the realm of the imagination, Rimbaud's "systematic derangement of the senses" rather than through direct action'.

To Doherty, Arcadia was 'The realm of the infinity...a poet's corner'. To those still not in the know, he described it as:

not a cult *or a religion – it'*s an awareness of your surroundings; you're not going to force yourself on anyone and, equally, no one's gonna force themselves on you. And it's about community and pleasure. It came from a whisper through the trees. It came from a crack *in the pavement. It can also come when you open a bag of crisps, or when you* kick *a* football *against a goalpost.*

Perhaps mindful of potential applications to Private Eye's Pseuds Corner being made on his behalf, Doherty added:

Even if I was winding you up, it would still be true, because Arcadia and the Arcadian Dream is so deep, is so true to our hearts...There have been Arcadian gatherings over the years, but I think the best is yet to come. It can be as powerful as your imagination can allow it to be. But, it can also be as dark and twisted as your soul...Arcadia encompasses the infinite, and that's why it comforts me.

Perhaps more usefully, he described also this mythology as 'the code by which we live our lives...the pact we've sworn all those years ago that turned us all from enemies into companions and wayfarers and travellers on the seas of Albion'. In Doherty-speak, this suggests that talk of Albion and Arcadia was part of an emotional dialect, lexis relevant to him and Barât. A reminder of a binding emotional pact made in youth.

The ambiguity of phrases advising that 'the best is yet to come' suggests an impulse to evoke a lost England using the band's various means of expression. In fitting with this, tracks such as *The Good Old Days* (itself evoking a lost England as with other tracks from *Up the Bracket*) would be furnished with lines such as:

If Queen Boadicea is long dead and gone
Still then the spirit in her children's children's children
Lives on.

Doherty, for all his drug addictions, toxic inter-band relationships and chaotic attitudes towards personal organisation, was capable of a compelling analysis of England. What's striking about the track he later released with post-Libertines outfit Babyshambles is how well, in 2005, he portrayed a changing Britain. With a northern region starved of government investment, its people left behind by globalisation whilst investment focused on the capital. He sings of how:

Down in Albion
They're black and blue
But we don't talk about that
Babyshambles, Down in Albion

The mournful, melancholy opening slips into an Arcadian reverie, evoking Waugh's sun-kissed garden lawns, with images of 'Gin in teacups / And leaves on the lawn'. This is sharply contrasted with images of violence at bus stops, violence in dole queues, and of 'pale thin girls with eyes forlorn', adopting a meter that evoked archaic poetry.

Doherty's dreams of escape, in the song, are nothing if not realistic. Perhaps mindful of the recent availability of £1 Megabus journeys he suggests:

We could go to
Deptford, Catford,
Watford, Digberth,
Mansfield.

All this is sung with enough wanderlust to suggest genuine longing. The contrast of 'pith helmets' and 'Reebok classics' suggests an artistic consciousness agile enough to visualise Albion as a Mobius strip of time, a seemingly continuous belt of references that in fact loops back on to itself. It's easy to laugh at his pretension, but neglectful to do so.

Doherty would find himself in and out of drug rehabilitation centres, post-Libertines. Matthew Pritchard, better known as the acoustic troubadour Lupen Crook, would also dwell in institutions during his ongoing struggles with schizoaffective disorder. A London-dwelling singer who counted Syd Barrett as an influence, Crook moved socially in the same orbit as The Libertines. But his songs would have an even darker vision of Albion.

In his single *Halloween*, he sang, 'It's a sign of the times I fear / blow out your brains / I'm fucked if I care'.

With other lines describing how he'd 'howl at the moon and bleed at the ears', Crook also evoked the madness of a frustrated youth, adrift from a sense of meaning in an age that seems to have left him behind.

Patrick Wolf would mark his emergence on to the scene with the startlingly eclectic, emotional and fractured album *Lycanthropy*. A thrilling ragbag of the acoustic and electronic, his debut charted his development from man to the Wolf of his moniker. With the album cover serving to reveal the references of his inner world, he posed as a soot-covered urchin – all long shorts and Victorian hoops. Crook and Wolf, with their Dickensian stage names and their keenness to adopt battered stringed instruments over ornate lyrics, would both suggest young male figures battered by the ruthless onslaught of modernisation. In *Pigeon Song* Wolf sang of attending cinemas alone and feeding pigeons day after day. He sounded both like an old man and an urchin who has snuck into the local 'picture house'. Wolf evokes the innocent bludgeoned by the city, by a modern age which demands too much of such sensitive souls, when he sings:

London
Did you have to take my child away?
You buried it under rent
And low pay.

Wolf's image of London shares with Billy Childish's poetry a tough honesty about the grit and desperation of the capital. Sharing with Wolf a visual appearance that is almost Dickensian, Childish describes the capital in the year 2000 with the weary detail of the crushingly familiar. In *Chatham Town Welcomes Desperate Men* Childish would talk of 'the indebted and the owners of nought' against a backdrop of 'salesman who never sell, the dentist who hates teeth, the docker without a dock and the robber of car hubcaps'. For all this awareness of London's hustle, lies and tough economic realities in the new decade, he would address the city not as something to be pleaded with, but as some kind of benign angel that embraces all. Despite its:

Grey skies and icy winds
Counsellors of little faith
Estate agents bearing false gifts

Childish concludes:

Chatham town welcomes desperate men
It loves you all and it honours you all.

This would evoke the words of The Libertines' debut *What A Waster*, which had the line 'the cities hard / the cities fair'. Childish's paintings have a visceral quality similar to the lyrics. Using thick acrylic paint it retains a bracing immediacy. With the enunciation of the Surrealists and the vibrant colours of the Post Impressionists he would influence young artists like Henry Hudson. In his piece *The Rise and Fall of Young Sen* Hudson would re-interpret Hogarth's eighteenth-century narrative *A Rake's Progress* using plasticine. Portraying scenes from Sen's life, Hudson would portray the present day in all its overpopulated, gory, commercial and nuanced glory.

By Patrick Wolf's second album, *The Wind in The Wires*, he was really focusing on what was missing from our culture. In *The Libertines* (a single which pressed the question of whether, like Doherty, he'd read the Marquis de Sade's *The Lust of The Libertines*) he sang of how 'all our heroes lack any conviction / they shout through the bars of cliché / and addiction'. That last line seemed to be a barb aimed at Doherty, in an age where even remaining male figureheads for the youth – such as David Beckham and Wayne Rooney – seemed unable to emerge from the torpor of commercialism to inspire their young with a coherent tournament performance on the world stage, the indulgences of wealth ill-preparing them for the pressure to achieve in maturity.

The lyrical trajectory of The Libertines, and Wolf, suggest an Albion running aground. Perhaps this could be partly attributed to the issue many of these artists were concerned with – that of men finding their feet in the present day, languishing instead in various states of addiction, immaturity or transition. Where the artistic male lacks for heroes as well as affordable housing – a *Time for Heroes*, indeed. When, on Wolf's second album, he retreated to the countryside and reflected that in songs about Teignmouth, the message seemed clear – the crushing burdens of contemporary London had defeated him.

Chapter 17

Pencil Skirts and Motorway Modernism – The Long Blondes and Black Box Recorder

If the artistic men of this era seemed to be battered by the present and soothed by nostalgia, the women in pop culture seemed to be utilising the idea of England to thrilling effect.

Black Box Recorder (a brainchild of Luke Haines from The Auteurs) would hit the top 20 with their breathy blend of pop and erotica titled *The Facts of Life.* In its attendant album Morrissey's sense of a layered England, teeming with secrets, was re-engaged. But where Morrissey sang of something 'black, absurd and hateful' at its heart, through Haines' mouthpiece Sarah Nixey England's hidden layers contained secret lust.

In *May Queen* even the school day English symbol of femininity is secretly imploring a boy to 'Meet me in the playground after school / promise not to breathe a word to anyone'. The sheer intensity of these hidden trysts is apparent in her demands that he 'write my name in blood across your shirt' as backing singers remind us this is the 'May Queen'. 'Kids can be so cruel,' she adds, as if aware this is a mere Fact Of Life.

Like The Long Blondes, Nixey and Black Box Recorder would sing of the thrill of the road. 'The English Motorway system is beautiful and strange,' Nixey sang, on a song written in tribute to it. Elsewhere the motorway is conveyed in an almost Ballardian way, as 'an accident waiting to happen', and once again, the erotic thrills of this land do not cover its constant sense of threat. Nor does it ensure the satisfaction of these thrills. 'There are things we need to talk about,' Nixey sings, adding, 'there are things I cannot do without.' The song leaves the listener to wonder at what perverse thrills our narrator is withholding from us. What is clearer is that where Paul Weller found clarity amongst the land's riverbanks, Haines finds it amongst the thrum and pulse of a motorway system that 'eliminates all diversions'. Like a Ballard character, his psyche had been warped by urban living. Nixey sang:

> *You achieve a zen-like state*
> *As someone else is driving*
> *Become detached*
> *Observing colours and straight lines*
> *Distant towns and exit signs*

In Nixey, Haines seemed to have found a personification for all his assumed assumptions about the unattainable woman. For all his lyrical skill and insight, these assumptions sometimes sounded a little too much like a man speaking through a woman. The hope seemed to be that affectless, icy vocals would gloss over any such flaws.

In Black Box Recorder, English femininity is not just about hidden lust and perversion. Name checking the beloved Lady Diana Spencer, the glacial track *The New Diana* uses Nixey to style some potent ideas about female aspiration. Sang from the perspective of a woman who is, 'A queen of hearts / now a mother' she sings, 'from one English rose to another / I want to be the new Diana'. Her planned trajectory is from local beauty contests to the national stage, and from there into the hearts and minds of the nation, as revealed by the lines:

> *Miss South of England*
> *Miss United Kingdom*

What is fascinating here is the subtle use of English mythology that is fluidly woven into a fleeting verse:

> *The heart that healed*

The hand that fed
Lady of the lake
Lady in red
Island in an island
In an island

To the song's protagonist, Diana was an island, living on the British Isles, who after death would be buried on a small island of her own. Even in a state of aspiration, the protagonist is aware of the isolated compartments that her success would entail.

Detailing what exactly her ambition would entail, she muses about, 'Lying on a yacht reading photo magazines / visiting the shore occasionally'. But there may be a more subversive intent behind the song. 'Where's the new republic?' she asks.

The Long Blondes (whose guitar lines were written by a man called Dorian) were, like their heroes Pulp, skilled bricoleurs. Singer Kate Jackson used the finest wares from the vintage shop she worked in to deck out her band. In so doing the band cast themselves amongst England's most evocative visual reference points as only pop stars can. Posing amongst the Mills & Boon section in Bethnal Green library in East London they appeared to have stepped out of the film noir classic *Double Indemnity*. There were neckerchiefs and pencil skirts for the women and pastel cardigans and tight 'slacks' for the boys. The Long Blondes described themselves as 'the ultimate fantasy pop group: Jean Harlow, Mae West, Edie Sedgwick, Nico, Nancy Sinatra and Barbara Windsor'. Their lyrics cited English models Erin O'Connor and Lily Cole, and the producer of the *Carry On* films, Peter Rogers.

It is worth noting that their reference points, though not defiantly English, were deeply in thrall to the *His 'n' Hers* era of that other great Sheffield band, Pulp. Owen Hatherley even described The Long Blondes as an 'all-dancing, all-adultery, all-acrylic tribute to *His 'n' Hers*'.

Acknowledging their indebtedness to British culture, Kate Jackson informed The Independent that, 'Dorian and I are obsessed with old British comedy films, and we were [just] watching *No Sex Please, We're British* with Ronnie Corbett.' But she revealingly added, 'The things you grow up with are a grounding.' If, like Wolf and Doherty, The Long Blondes looked to the past for comfort, they were also noted for being Modernist. 'Even the artwork's got clean lines,' Jackson said. As with the other bands mentioned here, cultural texts were of deep importance to this band. As Jackson sang on *Lust in the Movies*, 'all I have now with me / Are the records and the books that I own'. The sense of the bricoleur being a part of the bricolage was apparent.

Unlike Doherty, Jackson's wanderlust seemed to be less for a mythic England, or even the streets of London, but for escape altogether. In the thrilling *Separated by Motorways* she sang:

Separated by motorways
The A14 and the A1 (so long)
Separated by motorways
Two lonely girls go on the run

By the time of her debut solo single *Wonder Feeling* these sentiments would be further sharpened. Escape, to Jackson, was seemingly not just a physical act, or about the beauty and urban strangeness Black Box Recorder described, but also about mental clarity. But tellingly, it was an escape from work into the rich reference points of a modern England that Jackson craved. She sang of:

Life changing conversations
I'm in love with railway stations
Wonder feeling
Take me to the motorway

Can't find a reason
To go into work today

Escape, for Jackson and The Long Blondes, is not into the past, but into a sharply stylised present.

Chapter 18

Tennis Courts, Cellos and Yorkshire Valleys – Goldfrapp and My Summer of Love

My Summer of Love, the film adaptation of the Helen Cross novel, fuses aspects of contemporary English life and renders them with loving sensuality. This is a film with an eye for detail that only an obsessive – or an outsider – could muster. Polish director Pawel Pawlikowski allows the viewer to luxuriate in the richness of the spectacle during a film that burns with suburban – and subterranean – passion (the type that Pulp and The Long Blondes had perhaps made your average indie cinema goer familiar with). The film starts with the long, haunting notes of Goldfrapp's *Lovely Head*. The notes distorted in a manner that recalls seventies sci-fi theme tunes, topped with a breathy vocal to create a heady effect.

With the shimmering shots of Nathalie Press' character Mona, as she dips up and down Yorkshire hills on her bike, we are drawn into the very familiar fare of an English summer. Goldfrapp and Will Gregory were recruited to craft the soundtrack at a time when their work was most receptive to what Pawlikowski was trying to achieve. These musical partners were still in the mindset of their album *Seventh Tree*. It's a record on which idiosyncratic imagery of England – recalling May Balls and Pagan worship – was evocatively used in both artwork and video. On the album's cover, a Pierrot-like Goldfrapp rests her head against a figure wearing an oversized owl's head. It looks as if they are consoling one another after performing at some archaic English summer festival. Goldfrapp's aesthetic and musical preoccupations in this era were perfect for the purposes of the film.

Pawel Pawlikowski hunted far and wide across Yorkshire schools to cast Mona – the febrile Yorkshire redhead abandoned by her parents to live in a Yorkshire valley with her god-bothering brother. Just as the crime drama *Happy Valley* seemed set in an indiscriminate Yorkshire valley, sealed off from the modern world, so too the ruined pub that Mona lives in seems like a piece of detritus unmoored from its culture – thrown from the black hole of some seventies sitcom and on to our screen. Left to rot, with its ruined walls and forcefully emptied optics. Mona (played by Nathalie Press) is so bored and isolated – even from her brother – that she's left to scrawl self-portraits on the walls and feign suicide in order to get her brother's attention. This depiction of a young girl – adrift from the security of domestic structure, left at the mercy of a guardian with acute problems of their own, in a valley forgotten by time – is sadly all too plausible. England has, outside the media's London-centric eye – many of these places tucked away in its landscape. Whilst many of its residents may be unapologetic, or even proud of their isolation, one can only imagine the Monas left to rot in pockets of ruined Albion until adulthood sets them free. Their incendiary, uncultivated charisma and nascent sexuality are rocket fuel – truly dangerous in the wrong hands.

During a star-shaped sunbathe in long grass, Mona is discovered by Tamsin (played magnificently by Emily Blunt). When Mona reveals that her name is a pun on Mona Lisa, Tamsin counters that she 'studied the original'. Whilst Mona gets about on a motorbike with no engine Tamsin rides imperiously above her on a white horse, which allows her to first appear to Mona, saviour-like, from the sun. It is clear that Tamsin and Mona come from different ends of the social spectrum. Where Tamsin's days are elevated by the signifiers of the upper-middle classes (horses, tennis courts, croissants) Mona is left to make broken items work for her – most prominently her engineless bike (perhaps a neat figurative metaphor for her motor-less life).

When Mona first visits Tamsin at her house she is overawed by its splendour, and how it contrasts with her own home. Mona's house is a leaf-drenched Manor, complete with the buzzing of summer lawns. It is protected, as such palatial residences are, by a long driveway and by a thick crop of trees. With its exotic rugs and exposed wooden floors, the house has enough lavish, faintly ethnic interiors to evoke a distinct texture to the world Mona lives in. Where Mona's home induces attempted frustration and attempted suicide, the bay windows and four-poster beds of Tamsin's house afford her the room to develop rich mental interiors – and even indulgent fantasies (the one concerning a dead sister being the most divisive within the film).

On seeing Mona enter her home, Tamsin, with a small smile, ostentatiously completes her cello performance before greeting her, revelling in Mona's reaction to the spectacle. When she explains that she had just been playing Saint-Saens's *The Swan* on cello, Mona responds that she lives above a pub called The Swan. The extremes of the social spectrum the two of them exist in are neatly summarised in this exchange. Tamsin lives in an England in which pain also comes from being deprived – emotionally if not materially – by distant parents. Her mother is a ghostly presence, observed only by Mona through windows, and her father is more concerned with his young mistress. Recently suspended, and with her intellect left to fester over the summer, Tamsin finds in Mona a new plaything. This is the upper-middle classes dining on what they patronisingly deem the exuberant fare of the working classes. All too aware that when they tire of the game they can dismiss its characters and revert back to their padded lives. Mona's neglect is so absolute (one scene shows her being sexually used by a married man) that she sees in Tamsin a kindred spirit. Tamsin makes the most of the tools at her disposal – after a sleep-over she serves Tamsin croissants, juice and coffee in bed on a royal tray, as if it is all a matter of course for the likes of her. The two of them bathe topless in the garden, smoking, and frolic in a submerged lake in one of the leafy clefts of the valley. The soundtrack compels the viewer to join Mona during her immersion in this new-found, liminal realm of her village. Goldfrapp's echoing, isolated piano notes of the theme *Mona on the Tennis Court* and the plucked strings of *Meeting on the Moors* suggest finally found tranquillity of a psychedelic and potent kind. I mentioned Julian Palacios' (2010) argument that Syd Barrett spawned the English, psychedelic mindset with his depiction of fairy-tale creatures in river banks, as inspired by his time on the River Cam. It is a trope familiar enough for *My Summer of Love* to appropriate it as a touchstone.

The viewer becomes part of Mona's emotional journey. Goldfrapp's sensual vocals throughout the film remind us that summer – and its attendant indulgences – are ever present. Cross's novel starts with a line about the deathly heat and Pawlikowski ensures it stays ever-present visually, with long shots that capture the shimmering summer air.

The film uses two bounded settings that are deeply useful in terms of revealing character. The first has to be the trope of the English summer. Where the richness of the national identity, with parts of its spectrum over-invested and other parts under-invested, can be filleted quickly when events are on heat. The English summer – with its attendant, vague ideas of champagne and strawberries at Wimbledon, outdoor dips and long evenings on sunlit lawns – is a bounded idea in which both characters can experience revelry with there being a firm closing time. Namely – the inevitable resumption of school term for Tamsin.

The second bounded setting is through the use of the geographical environment – the English valley. Somewhere in the north of England, a setting attractive enough for the rich to have homes but remote enough for the isolation to be absolute and allow the characters to mine their own fantasies. The use of the 'valley' is a neat tool by which to examine a microcosm of England with enough precision for the journey to be satisfying for the viewer. The TV series *Happy Valley* would later portray this in a dystopian manner, showing the lawlessness of an England in which the state not just allows but actually encourages psychopathy to run free (with the empathic types being left to pick up the pieces given state underfunding). In *My Summer of Love* it is not criminality which is explored so much as feverish adolescent sexuality. If the lesbianism between the two leads is neither convincing nor voyeuristic then we get the sense – with the fine directorial brushstrokes – that it is not supposed to be. It is all part of a sensual dive into the inner worlds of these young women.

Mona and Tamsin together reclaim the valley – appropriating Albion's secluded lakes as their own rock-lined playground. When they find magic mushrooms and take them, before gate-crashing a local dance, this is the English youth reclaiming the rituals of the older generation with mocking exuberance. Here, Goldfrapp's music is at its most potent, with the young couple shocking the adults around them with their flirting. Revealing the hedonism that their utter isolation has gifted them.

Devoid of meaningful occupations the two are gleeful in disrupting the aged social traditions of the valley, in shaking up the way things are. The occupants of the valley – who Pawlikowski portrays as being easily led by Mona's brother – come across as sheep-like. They are either sleepily docile or unselfconsciously aggressive – they have also been left behind. The temptations of cultish Christianity, alcohol, the occult, and illicit sex suggest this is a valley that has been so far left behind that it is trying to anaesthetise itself from resultant pain with fleeting pleasure. When Tamsin lures the soft-hearted Mona into a séance – ostensibly to summon the ghost of her dead sister – Mona is scared; her natural empathy makes her vulnerable in the hands of a girl like Tamsin. But what the bourgeoisie Tamsin *really* fears is not the other side, but boredom. The opportunity to have to face her own inner world which is itself neglected, too long buttressed by the temporary luxuries of her class. The fact that both of them will be scorched by the activities of the summer is all par for the course when the ruling classes are bored with an England that they carved up.

Chapter 19

Non-Place and Negative Space – Gazelle Twin and JG Ballard

By 2014 the idea of a romantic England seemed harder to evoke. The Brighton-based artist Gazelle Twin conveyed, in her debut album *The Entire City*, the sense that intense industrialisation and gentrification would never succeed in marshalling the forces of nature, which would always come to eventually reclaim the land. Influenced by the nuanced dioramas of German artist Max Ernst, and the apocalyptic visions in JG Ballard's writing her work seemed to offer warnings regarding the direction industrialisation takes us in. Perhaps more than any artist mentioned so far, Gazelle Twin's work captures the Ballardian essence.

In novels such as *The Drowned World*, the Shepperton-based Ballard presented a vision of London submerged by flooding. By combining the familiar with the fantastical to eerie effect he created a state of unease in the reader, to make them question the durability of their contemporary living environments. In later works, such as *High Rise*, Ballard portrayed gated communities, inspired by developments in countries such as Qatar. But Ballard's narratives always portrayed how the ugliness of people's ids would never be satiated by luxury and would combine with the forces of nature to overwhelm such settings.

In the video for her single *Anti Body* (from the 2014 album *Unflesh*) the Gazelle Twin 'performs' against a repeated five-note drum motif that does not develop throughout the song. In the video her hooded, masked character spends the duration in an underground, dim-lit and dirty subterranean space. The character at once commands the space, with her idiosyncratic dancing, and yet also seems trapped in it (an effect enhanced by the evoked claustrophobia of the close-miked singing). This character seems to be evolving, through her movements, a private coping strategy in this secluded space, idiosyncratic enough to be disturbing. Ian Curtis' spasmodic movements are evoked, begging the question of whether extreme industrialisation, and the liminal zones it leaves in its wake, leave occupants in a catatonic state. The performance space is, nonetheless, a living space, with its own shower and changing rooms (even if this 'living space' seems more a hellish netherworlds than a functional setting. It certainly lacks the glossy glamour of the landscapes depicted in popular R&B videos). If R&B interiors often invoke sumptuous settings conducive for the amorous, Gazelle Twin takes us to the other extreme.

It is an interior similar to that evoked by *One Hundred Years*, a space for deeply negative and private emotional expression to also be expressed outside the realm of normal life. The characters residence in it seems illustrative of an unresolvable emotional state, 'negative space' rendered actual through the medium of video. Where Smith sang of how 'something small falls out of your mouth and we laugh', here insects crawl up the walls. The video is certainly Gothic in its evocation of a disintegrating space in which nature is reclaiming (as in the cover for *Disintegration*). In opening up a negated geographical landscape Gazelle Twin creates art in the Gothic vein of The Cure.

Through these different forms of musical negation both artists seem to be creating an alternative conceptual room (responding to the lack of a 'free space' which Bottà described) to construct a space, through video graphic sleight of hand, on their chosen terms. For Gazelle Twin negation is not just about the removal of domestic functioning, but is of itself a fertile space for new expression and, possibly, a hint of where life may be heading. In an interview with the author, Gazelle Twin was questioned about whether she is drawn to aspects of art which some might consider 'negative'. She answered:

Totally. I find it incredibly satisfying. I get off on really intense atmospheres...maybe it just comes back to this thing about how our environment shapes us. Whatever we grow up with dictates our needs and experiences as an adult – good and bad.

Gazelle Twin seemed to use her videos to represent the urban, functionally-deprived environment she felt abandoned in, truthfully representing that actual, but seemingly 'negative' space as an expression of her needs.

Bernholz, in the same interview, evoked the postmodern disintegration described in works by JG Ballard (such as *Concrete Island*). She talked of:

...enjoying the feeling of being in clinical, non-places. Car parks, harshly lit waiting rooms etc. The more luminous the lighting, the more run down the better too, because that's when you see the cracks exposed.

This use of Marc Auge's term 'non-places' is insightful, opening up as it does the possibility that she sought to deliberately reclaim these spaces in her work. In it these negated, deprived spaces are useful to her, as they expose cracks in the postmodern façade. In our interview Bernholz explained how she intended to reclaim the hell of school changing rooms, a reality that was disturbing enough for her that as a teenager she developed Body Dysmorphic Disorder. She explained how, by using these landscapes from her childhood, she was reclaiming them as well as returning to them.

Elsewhere in our interview she justified her sampling of the supermarket 'beat' as a repetitive, percussive tool in her song *Belly of the Beast*. She said:

First off I heard this bleep sound in Sainsbury's and when

they're all running together you sometimes get the odd harmony or chord...Supermarkets are busy, frantic places of desire, domination, class, greed etc...it feels like a microcosm of modern capitalism – all the really bad shit under one roof.

So it seems that the textscapes and landscapes in which negation was captured were in fact more than a personal or even conceptual expression, and closer to a state of the nation manifesto. Bernholz was depicting life in the underbelly of the corporate beast (when the branch of a franchise has been hastily relocated perhaps) with the blasted interiors, the ruined electrics, the insect-infested consequences of aggressive capital.

In 2014, in an increasingly urban Britain where light-touch regulation allowed corporate companies increasing power, it did feel time to sound the alarm. The alienation that Gary Numan and Ian Curtis had presciently evoked had come to pass. When Bernholz sang, in *Human Touch*, of 'living inside / a simulation' it was hard to disagree with the sense that in 2014 England felt more like a hologram of a past country. A deadened country that existed now only in past representations, now little more than a series of strip-lit consumerist sites, connected by a brutally efficient web of motorways.

The governmental imperative seemed to be to push its inhabitants to consume as much as possible because if the economy kept expanding then those in power got to stay in power. A backdrop of increasing globalisation added another aspect to the alienation, demanding as it did deeper investment in technology at the expense of human vocation. On a personal level, our entrenched relationships with technology seemed to serve often to further alienate ourselves from one another. Media technology, after all, was built to help people consume and re-consume their experiences by reproducing them repeatedly. Alienation was becoming a more overtly layered phenomenon.

Chapter 20

Looking for Albion

Given the possibility of addressing these concerns, one persistent criticism of the left has been its inability to offer a coherent alternative to the centre-right, which has dominated politics in recent years. The rise of Jeremy Corbyn as a cult figure, who prompted massive chanting to the tune of *Seven Nation Army*, brought discourse about the left to the fore. In 2019 the criticism remained that Michael Foot's socialist ideas from the 1970s were merely being rehashed in Corbyn's vision. With the perceived failure of Labour to offer a coherent answer to Brexit and their perceived failure to deal with the smear of anti-Semitism, Corbyn's vision for England was buried in the Conservatives 2019 election landslide. But what exactly was Corbyn's vision? An England with a 4-day week, an allotment dwelling, jam-making England, which looks to South American countries for moral examples? A more compassionate, Socialist England? Or was it as simple as the fact that Corbyn's scruffiness smacked too much of the scuzzy seventies counterculture for most of the electorate, and Johnson's scruffiness reminded the electorate of the quintessential naughty school boy – which they could live with? One only has to look at some members of Johnson's cabinet to wonder if the trust the electorate has with such 'naughty schoolboys' is solid. Jacob Rees-Mogg, whose entire persona seems to defer to a nineteenth-century aesthetic and Beano-esque schtick, when pressed seems ready to overrule any tradition – from the monarchy to the Speaker of the House – if it suits his political aims. His genuine lack of respect for the status quo was even apparent in his revealingly controversial statement that victims of Grenfell should have ignored evacuation advice. The point is, the likes of Rees-Mogg and Johnson know how to appear familiar, naughty and establishment-like until their personas are scratched. Is the deference to the norm offered by Johnson's cabinet in fact more of an appropriation of the norm as protection? As a shield which masks an unbreakable – and very cold – self-belief underneath it?

It may well be the case that Corbyn's vision was simply too radical. That an electorate pummelled by uncertainty, in a Brexit climate that the Conservatives had fostered out of their own fear of the far right, were not brave enough to plump for Corbyn's vision. It seems fitting that a volume that began with Just William should end with Boris Johnson, whose bumbling persona seems to tap into an enduring English affection for vague ideas of the 'scoundrel'. If rumours of Johnson's private behaviour mark him as in fact something far more sinister, then in uncertain times, for all their tolerance of rebels and outsiders, the English seem to have chosen the devil they know.

This is all the more remarkable given the failure of the Conservative government to offer credible narratives on the future of the NHS, youth housing and student debt. This doubt has led the youth to rally to the left (albeit not in significant enough numbers to permit a left-wing governmental coalition). The right argues that realistically there isn't the funding to address such issues, that taxes will have to rise. The left retorts that this concern is itself a ploy from the ideological right. In a post-truth age there is a sense that political rhetoric has less substance than ever. In an age where music and books have become more digital there can also be the sense that they too have less substance – but that is wrong. They exist within the privacy of people's consciousness with more diversity than ever. In an era where Johnson's perceived untrustworthiness seems to be seen as less of an issue than the appeal of his gung-ho patriotism it appears that deeper affections in the British mentality are enduring. The British electorate, at present, seem to prefer voting into power a party that has been proven to lie to them to taking a risk on an unproven alternative. Jeremy Hunt, when Conservative Party Secretary of State for Health, was widely proven to have misrepresented NHS statistics about the so-called 'Weekend Effect' but this was not deemed by the electorate as damning enough to deny his party a majority in 2019.

If the left manage a coherent response under a new leader – one which combines the sleek aesthetic of the centre ground with the radical socialism espoused by Corbyn – they might yet harness the enthusiasm of the young whilst offering a credible alternative. The cynics argue that Johnson's victory is a death-knell for liberal ideas. Hugh Grant claims that the country is finished, and it is striking to see the actor who played lead roles in so many rose-tinted portrayals of Albion saying that.

But perhaps England is not finished – it just needs to take hold of the future. It no longer needs to rehash seventies counterculture or indulge in colonial nostalgia. Britain can be reinvigorated, and express deeper, more nourishing undercurrents that prevail within it. The sense of interclass cooperation fostered in the Second World War, combined with the individual agency and talent that made Sherlock Holmes such a recognisably English character. The success of artistic collectives like Massive Attack. In this collection I have elucidated the cultural moments in which overlooked demographics through invention, talent and sheer force of ambition have incorporated their worldview into the mass consciousness, benefiting us all as a result. I have looked at how artistic collectives have formed springboards for rich artistic careers, creating rich seams of inspiration for future generations. All these qualities could be expressed in Britain's shop front window – in its leaders as well as in its artists – making it a country proud of its nature, no longer ashamed of it. Britain's navel gazing nostalgia could be a thing of the past, along with its tendency to self-sabotage. Michael Bracewell wrote of the angry youth, distrustful of a modern England which he saw as 'strangled by consumerism on one hand and political failure on the other'. In truth, the fragmentation of urban living will not stop until a generation is prepared to forgo ongoing economic prosperity in favour of the nuances of a better quality of life. Not in material terms, but in human terms. It is quite probable that the Millennial prioritisation of the environment could be the engine for that change, and could lead to a stronger sense of moral leadership in the political class once the next generation are finally in post. No longer will the high street and the village be further atomised in favour of increased commercial possibility. No longer will urban living become increasingly atomised in the way Gazelle Twin described. The risk of environmental catastrophe could lead to a right angle in the path the country takes, with the collective will required inspiring a turn back towards a sense of responsibility within the community. This change could be enriched by insights from component members of a metropolitan, multi-racial, inclusive country, with the wealth of experience they offer the country.

For all that, in early 2020 Corbyn might be deemed a failure on his own terms, he did lead his party to being one with the largest membership of any in Europe. And, lest it be forgotten, for all his public-school education Corbyn is a collective figurehead for the long-lost English counterculture. The fact that he did not achieve high office is perhaps not remarkable. It is not simply that the English cannot tolerate rebels – it is perhaps that they tolerate a kind of sanctioned rebellion that they can be sure will not jeopardise their own patch. But with statistics from the last election showing that the youth are far left in mindset, this sense of nimbyism cannot last for long, unless the youth shift to the right in a manner they are not known to do. Can the uneasy truce that the electorate have struck with a Conservative party that they do not trust last long after the Brexit issue has been addressed? Perhaps PJ Harvey put it best when she said 'let England shake'.

References

Prologue
Bracewell, M. (1998) *England is Mine*, London, Flamingo Books.

Chapter 1 Ginger Beer in Teacups, and Leaves on the Lawn – Oscar Wilde, Just William, Sherlock Holmes and The Age of Innocence

Wilde, O. (2003) *The Complete Works of Oscar Wilde*. London, Collins.

Bracewell, M. (1998) *England is Mine*. London, Flamingo Books.

Disher, M. (1990) *Growing up with Just William: Richmal Crompton's Niece Tells the Inside Family Story*. London, The Outlaws Publishing Company.

Crompton, R. (1999) *William Does His Bit*. London, Macmillan Children's Books.

The Prisoner (1967) BBC1 29 September.

Crompton, R. (1998) *William the Detective*. London, Macmillan Children's Books.

Sherlock Holmes and the Voice of Terror (1942) Directed by John Rawlins [Film]. New York, Universal Pictures.

Conan Doyle, A. (1887) *A Study in Scarlet*. London, Ward Lock and Co.

Chapter 2 Bedazzled in Soho – from Evelyn Waugh to Shelagh Delaney and Peter Cook

Waugh, E. (1928) *Decline and Fall*. London, Chapman and Hall.

Bracewell, M. (1998) *England is Mine*. London, Flamingo Books.

Waugh, E. (1945) *Brideshead Revisited, The Sacred & Profane Memories of Charles Ryder*. London, Chapman & Hall.

Waugh, E. (2012 ed) *Unconditional Surrender*. New York, Hachette USA.

Delaney, S. (1959). A Taste of Honey. London, Bloomsbury.

Peter Cook on Person to Person in 1979 (2019) YouTube video, added by Johnny Revolver [Online]. Available at https://www.youtube.com/watch?v=9Ur0OTsVoMM (Accessed 12 February 2020).

Thompson, H. (1997) *Peter Cook: A Biography*. London, Hodder and Stoughton.

Miller, J. (1961) 'Can English Satire Draw Blood?' *The Observer*, 1 October.

Chapter 3 Astronauts of Inner Space – Syd Barrett, Nick Drake and The Birth of Psychedelia

Drake, N. (1969) *Five Leaves Left* [CD]. London, Island Records.

Drake, N. (1971) *Bryter Later* [CD]. London, Island Records.

Humphries, P. (1997) *Nick Drake: The Biography*. London, Bloomsbury.

Palacios, J. (2010) *Syd Barrett & Pink Floyd*. London, Plexus.

The Verve. (1997) *Urban Hymns* [CD]. London, Hut.

The Verve. (1993) *A Storm in Heaven* [CD]. London, Hut.

Pink Floyd. (1967) *The Piper at the Gates of Dawn* [CD]. London, EMI.

Pink Floyd. (1969) *This Is Pink Floyd* [CD]. London, EMI.

Barrett, S. (1970) *Barrett* [CD]. London, Harvest.

Barrett, S. (1970) *The Madcap Laughs* [CD]. London, Harvest.

Barrett, S. (1988) *Opel* [CD]. London, Harvest.

Chapter 4 Velvet Goldmines – David Bowie, Lindsay Kemp and Kate Bush

Bowie, D. (1973) *Images 1966-1967* [CD]. London, Harvest.

Bowie, D. (1967) *David Bowie* [CD]. London, Dream Records.

Trynka, D. (2011) *Starman: The Definitive Biography*. Sphere, London.

Bowie, D. (1972) *The Rise and Fall of Ziggy Stardust and The Spiders from Mars* [CD]. London, RCA.

Flowers: A Pantomime for Jean Genet by Lindsay Kemp (1968).

Directed by Lindsay Kemp [Edinburgh Festival, Edinburgh. 20 June 1968].

Bush, K. (1978) *Wuthering Heights* [CD]. London, EMI.

Wuthering Heights (1978) BBC 1, 24 September.

Bowie, D. (1969) *Space Oddity* [CD]. London, Parlophone.

Hebdige, D. (1979) *Subculture: The Meaning of Style*, London, Routledge.

Whiteley, S. (1999) *Sexing the Groove: Popular Music and Gender*. London: Routledge.

Chapter 5 Disco Lento and The New Europeans – Depeche Mode, Ultravox and Hurts

Bowie, D. (1977) *Low* [CD]. London, RCA.

Reynolds, S. (2005) *Rip It Up and Start Again: Post Punk 1978-1984*. Faber & Faber, Croydon.

Pyzik, A. (2014) *Poor but Sexy: Culture Clashes, Europe East and West*. Zer0 Books, Hants.

Depeche Mode (1983) *Everything Counts* [CD]. London, Mute Records.

Lange, S., and Burmeister, D. (2013) *Monument*, Aufbau Berlag, Berlin.

Ultravox (1977) *Ha! Ha! Ha!* [CD]. London, Island.

Ultravox (1980) *Vienna* [CD]. London, Chrysalis.

Hurts (2010) *Wonderful Life* [CD]. London, RCA.

Chapter 6 Catching That Butterfly – Alan Sillitoe, Paul Weller and Liza Radley

The Jam (1980) *Going Underground* [CD]. London, Polydor.

Grahame, K. (1908) *The Wind in the Willows*. London, Methuen.

The Jam (1980) *Sound Affects* [CD]. London, Polydor.

Wells, S. (2019) 'Excerpt: In Echoed Steps: The Jam and a Vision of Albion', 3:AM Magazine, 13 March [Online]. Available at https://www.3ammagazine.com/3am/extract-echoed-steps-jam-vision-albion/ (Accessed 12 February 2020).

Alan Sillitoe (1959) *The Loneliness of the Long-Distance Runner.* W.H. Allen, London.

Saturday Night, Sunday Morning (1960) Directed by Karel Reisz Bryanston [Film]. London, Bryanston Film.

Fletcher, T. (1979) 'The Jam in '79', Jamming! A New Reality for the Noughties' [Online]. Available at https://www.ijamming. net/Jammingmagazine/TheJam1979.html (Accessed 12 February 2020).

Chapter 7 Interzones, Edgelands, Psykick Dancehalls and Shamans – Gary Numan, Joy Division and Mark E Smith

Tubeway Army (1979) *Replicas* [CD]. London, Beggars Banquet.

Joy Division (1979) *Unknown Pleasures* [CD]. London, Factory Records.

Giacomo Bottà. (2005) 'Dancing to Architecture: Popular Music, Economic Crisis and Urban Change in 1980's Industrial Europe'. Serbian Architectural Journal, vol. 1, pp. 113-131.

Hall, S. (1986). 'On postmodernism and articulation: An Interview with Stuart Hall'. Journal of Communication Inquiry, vol. 10, no. 2, pp. 45-60.

Hatherley, O. *'From Rock to Rubble: How Manchester Lost Its Music'.* Available at: http://www.youtube.com/watch?v=Sc3-1U1ZxHA (Accessed 10 November 2012).

Foxx, J. (1980) *Underpass* [CD]. London, Virgin.

Phillips, S. (2014). 'Photographer Kevin Cummins' Best Shot'. Guardian, 2 October [Online]. Available at: http://www. theguardian.com/artanddesign/2011/oct/02/photograph-kevin-cummins-best-shot (Accessed 14 May 2014).

Beckett, A. (2010). *When The Lights Went Out.* Faber & Faber, London.

Savage, J. and Kureishi, H. (2005) *The Faber Book of Pop.* Faber & Faber, London.

Savage, J. (2009) *The England's Dreaming Tapes.* Faber & Faber,

London.

Mark Fisher (2013) *Ghosts of My Life*: *Writings on Depression, Hauntology and Lost Futures*. Zer0 Books, Hants.

Simpson, D. (2018). '"Diana's funeral" re-enacted in Salford with Jill Dando and a mariachi band', Guardian, 13 September [Online]. Available at: https://www.theguardian.com/ artanddesign/2018/sep/13/diana-funeral-re-enacted-salford-jill-dando-mariachi-band-princess-wales (Accessed 14 May 2014).

Welcome to the Candy Vortex (2019). Vimeo video, added by Chris Egon Searle [Online]. Available at: https://vimeo. com/252950842 (Accessed 12 February 2020).

The Valley of the Dolls (1967) Directed by Mark Robson [Film]. New York, 20th Century Fox.

The Fall (1979) *Dragnet* [CD]. London. Step-Forward.

The Fall (2007) *Reformation Post TLC* [CD]. London, Slogan Records.

Krippner, S. (2020). 'Jim Morrison: A Failed Shaman?' Centro de Estudios, 10 February [Online]. Available at: http://www. ceoniric.cl/jim-morrison-a-failed-shaman/ (Accessed 14 February 2020).

The Fall (1986) *Bend Sinister* [CD]. London, Beggars Banquet.

Joy Division Documentary: Ian's Past Regression Therapy (2003). YouTube video, added by Vaughan Walton [Online]. Available at: https://www.youtube.com/watch?v=FjK67CvCscg (Accessed 12 February 2020).

Joy Division (1980) *Warsaw* [CD]. MPG, Manchester.

Joy Division (1988) *Substance* [CD]. Factory, Manchester.

Smith, B. (2016) *The Rise, The Fall and The Rise*. Faber & Faber, London.

Pet Shop Boys (1984) *West End Girls* [CD]. London, Bobcat Records.

Chapter 8 Beyond the Boundaries of Pop and Rebellion – The Jimmy Savile Scandal

Mark Fisher (2013) *Ghosts of My Life: Writings on Depression, Hauntology and Lost Futures*. Zer0 Books, Hants.

Davies, D. (2014) *In Plain Sight: The Life and Lies of Jimmy Savile*. Quercus, London.

Savile, J. (1974) *As It Happens*. Barrie and Jenkins, London.

Orr, D. (2012) 'Jimmy Savile was an emperor with no clothes – and a celebrity cloak'. Guardian, 2 November [Online]. Available at: https://www.theguardian.com/commentisfree/2012/nov/02/jimmy-savile-emperors-new-clothes (Accessed 14 May 2014).

BBC News (2016) 'Lord Janner should have been prosecuted 25 years ago'. BBC, 20 January [Online]. Available at: https://www.bbc.co.uk/news/uk-england-leicestershire-35361376 (Accessed 14 February 2014).

Chapter 9 Under the Fridge – from Stephen Fry to Caroline Aherne, Johnny Vegas and James Acaster

Blackadder (1983) BBC 1, 15 June.

Citizen Smith (1977) BBC 1, 12 April.

Pennington, M. (2014) *Becoming Johnny Vegas*. Harper Collins, London.

John Shuttleworth Pigeons in Flight (1993). YouTube video, added by Popitinpete [Online]. Available at: https://www.youtube.com/watch?v=GXp455mQ4xE (Accessed 12 February 2020).

Peep Show (2003) Channel 4, 28 January.

The Royle Family (1998) BBC, 28 January.

I'm Alan Partridge (1997) BBC 2, 3 November.

The Office (2001) BBC 2, 9 July.

Derek (2012) Channel 4, 28 January.

Shooting Stars (1995) BBC 2, 28 January.

Alfie (1966) Directed by Lewis Gilbert Paramount [Film].

London, Paramount Pictures.

Bracewell, M. (1998) *England is Mine*, London, Flamingo Books.

Shooting Stars Showdown (2010). YouTube video, added by Brian Gittins [Online]. Available at: https://www.youtube.com/watch?v=QodEpTQaWlY (Accessed 12 February 2020).

James Acaster's Classic Scrapes (2010). YouTube video, added by The Podcast Lab [Online]. Available at: https://www.youtube.com/watch?v=IsooyRHnzVw (Accessed 12 February 2020).

Chapter 10 The Moors and Man About the House – Morrissey's Psychogeographic England

Hall, R. (2014 ed) *The Well of Loneliness*, Wordsworth Editions, London.

Savile, J. (1974) *As It Happens*, Barrie and Jenkins, London.

Man About the House (1973) ITV, 28 January.

Pet Shop Boys (1984) *West End Girls* [CD]. London, Bobcat Records.

The Smiths (1984) *The Smiths* [CD]. London, Rough Trade.

The Smiths (1986) *The Queen Is Dead* [CD]. London, Rough Trade.

Headley, J. (2019) '13 Songs for Halloween: Suffer Little Children by The Smiths', Kexp, 15 November [Online]. Available at: https://www.kexp.org/read/2019/10/15/13-songs-halloween-suffer-little-children-smiths/ (Accessed 14 May 2014).

Florrie Forde's Dear Old Blighty (2010). YouTube video, added by WW1 Photos [Online]. Available at: https://www.youtube.com/watch?v=nRsO7tCjhAA (Accessed February 12 2020).

The Smiths (1987) *Strangeways Here We Come* [CD]. London, Rough Trade.

Morrissey (1987) *Viva Hate* [CD]. London, HMV.

Morrissey (1992) *Your Arsenal* [CD]. London, Sire / Reprise.

Morrissey (1991) *Kill Uncle* [CD]. London, EMI.

Morrissey (1994) *Vauxhall And I* [CD]. London, Parlophone.

Greene, G. (1938) *Brighton Rock*, William Heinemann Ltd, London.

Morrissey (1997) *Maladjusted* [CD]. London, Sire / Island.

O' Hagan, S. (2019). 'So Much To Answer For' The Observer, 6 May [Online]. Available at: http://tiptopwebsite.com/ websites/index2.php?username=thesmithsfile&page=58 (Accessed 14 May 2014).

Morrissey (2002) *You Are The Quarry* [CD]. London, Attack / Sanctuary.

Chapter 11 Victoriana, Candlesticks and Mist – The Cure and the Art of Negation

Siouxsie And The Banshees (1991) *Face To Face* [CD]. London, UMC / CD.

Mueller, C.A. (2008) The Music of the Goth Subculture: Postmodernism and Aesthetics.

Mueller, C.A. The Music of the Goth Subculture: Postmodernism and Aesthetics.

The Cure (1989) *Disintegration* [CD]. London, Fiction.

The Cure (1982) *Pornography* [CD]. London, Fiction.

The Cure (1983) *Japanese Whispers* [CD]. London, Fiction.

Eliot, TS (1929) *Old Possum's Book of Practical Cats*. Faber & Faber, London.

The La's (1990) *The La's* [CD]. London, Go Discs / Polydor.

Chapter 12 Pigs, Riots and Taffeta – Brett Anderson's Blakeian Visions

Suede (1997) *Sci Fi Lullabies* [CD]. London, Nude Records.

The Kinks (1967) *Something Else by The Kinks* [CD]. PRT Records, London.

Bowie, D. (1972) *The Rise and Fall of Ziggy Stardust and The Spiders from Mars* [CD]. London, RCA.

Blur (1994) *Parklife* [CD]. London, Food Records.

Madness (1983) *Madness* [CD]. London, Geffen.

Dixon Of Dock Green (1960). YouTube video, added by Spondonman [Online]. Available at: https://www.youtube.

com/watch?v=1tQRglQqyf8 (Accessed 12 February 2020).

Suede (1993) *Suede* [CD]. London, Nude Records.

Suede (1994) *Dog Man Star* [CD]. London, Nude Records.

Bowie, D. (1974) *David Live* [CD]. London, RCA Records.

The Libertines (2002) *Up the Bracket* [CD]. London, Rough Trade.

Barnett, D. (2003) *Suede: Love and Poison: The Official Biography.* Andre Deutsch, London.

Anderson, B. (2019) *Afternoons with the Blinds Drawn.* Little, Brown, London.

Suede (2016) *Night Thoughts* [CD]. London, Warner Music.

Chapter 13 The Other Morrissey – Paul Gascoigne, TFI Friday and Ladettes

Man About the House (1973) ITV, 28 January.

Fantasy Football League (1994) BBC2, 14 January.

TFI Friday (1996) Channel 4, 9 February.

My Summer with Des (1998) BBC, 25 May.

Chapter 14 Feather Boas and Crimplene – Pulp, Romo, Placebo, Velvet Goldmine and PJ Harvey

Warman, C.R. (1969) *Sheffield: Emerging City*, City Engineer and Surveyor and Town Planning Officer, London.

Sheffield: City on the Move (2015) YouTube video, added by Simon Norman [Online]. Available at: https://www.youtube.com/watch?v=-v1-mT9afP4(Accessed 12 February 2020).

Hatherley, O. (2011) Uncommon: An Essay on Pulp. Zero Books, Winchester.

Pulp (1994) *His 'n' Hers* [CD]. Island, London.

Pulp (1995) *Different Class* [CD]. Island, London.

Benjamin, W. (2002) *The Arcades Project.* Harvard University Press, Harvard.

Pulp (1987) *Freaks* [CD]. Fire Records, London.

Pulp (1993) *Lipgloss* [CD]. Island Records, London.

Pulp (1998) *This Is Hardcore (Deluxe Edition)* [CD], London.

Gilloch, G. (1997) *Myth and Metropolis: Walter Benjamin and The City*, Polity, London.

Romo Scene on Japanese TV (1995) feat. Minty, Simon Price, Viva (2015). YouTube video, added by Simon Price [Online]. Available at: https://www.youtube.com/ watch?v=Kj9k4ZP2e7U (Accessed 20 February 2020).

Simpson, D. (2000) 'The Scenes That Time Forgot', The Observer, 6 May [Online]. Available at: https://www.theguardian.com/ music/2009/aug/06/forgotten-music-scenes (Accessed 14 May 2014).

Velvet Goldmine (1998) Directed by Todd Haynes [Film]. London, Channel 4 Films.

Placebo (2003) *Sleeping with Ghosts* [CD]. Hut, London.

Placebo (1996) *Placebo* [CD]. Hut, London.

Placebo (1998) *Pure Morning* [CD]. London.

Genet, J. (1943) *Lady of the Flowers*. Marc Barbezat – L'Arbalete, Paris.

Day, C. (2019). 'Corrinne Day Photographer' Corrinne Day Online, 11 February [Online]. Available at: https://www. corinneday.co.uk/sets/297/ (Accessed 14 May 2014).

Harvey, PJ. (1991) *Dry* [CD]. Too Pure, London.

Harvey, PJ. (1994) *Rid of Me* [CD]. Island, London.

Harvey, PJ. (1995) *To Bring You My Love* [CD]. Island, London.

Harvey, PJ. (1997) *Is This Desire?* [CD]. Island, London.

Shreibak, N. (2017). 'The Many Faces of Polly Jean Harvey's Evolution in Fashion & Music' Hooligan Magazine, 11th July [Online]. Available at: http://www.hooliganmagazine.com/ blog/2017/7/11/the-many-faces-of-polly-jean-pj-harveys-evolution-in-fashion-music (Accessed 14 May 2014).

Tricky (1998) *Angels with Dirty Faces* [CD]. Island, London.

Harvey, P. (2011) *Let England Shake,* [CD]. Island, London.

Bowie, D. (1970) *The Man Who Sold the World* [CD]. Mercury Records, London.

Bowie, D. (1972) *The Rise and Fall of Ziggy Stardust And The Spiders from Mars* [CD]. RCA, London.

Chapter 15 Ghosts, Hauntings and Mezzanines – Massive Attack, Tricky, Dizzee Rascal and Stormzy

Massive Attack (1991) *Blue Lines* [CD]. Wild Bunch / Virgin, London.

Culture Fandom (2017) 'Unfinished Sympathy' Culture Fandom, 11 July [Online]. Available at: https://culture.fandom.com/wiki/Unfinished_Sympathy (Accessed 14 May 2014).

Tricky (1995) *Maxinquaye* [CD]. Island, London.

Harvey, PJ. (1997) *Is This Desire?* [CD]. Island, London.

Tricky (1996) *Pre-Millennium Tension*, [CD]. Island, London.

Fisher, M. (2014) Ghosts of My Life: Writings on Depression, Hauntology and Lost Futures. Zer0 Books, Winchester.

Japan (1982) *Ghosts* [CD]. Virgin, London.

Bladerunner (1982) Directed by Ridley Scott [Film]. New York, Warner Bros.

The Valley of the Dolls (1967) Directed by Mark Robson [Film]. New York, 20th Century Fox.

The Specials (1981) *Ghost Town* [CD]. 2 Tone Records, London.

Massive Attack (1998) *Mezzanine* [CD]. Circa / Virgin Records, London.

Goldie (1994) *Inner City Life* [CD]. London Music Stream / Because Music, London.

Goldie (1998) *Temper, Temper* [CD]. FFRR, London.

Dizzee Rascal (2003) *Boy in da Corner* [CD]. XL, London.

Chapter 16 Dickensian Pop and Arcady – The Libertines, Queen Boadicea, Patrick Wolf and Billy Childish

Barât, C. (2010) *Three Penny Memoir: The Lives of A. Libertine.* Fourth Estate, London.

Welsh, P. (2011) *Kids in the Riot: High and Low With The Libertines*, Omnibus Press, London.

Zulu (1964) Directed by Cy Endfield [Film]. London, Diamond Films.

Doherty, P. (2019). 'Quotes' Tutor Net, 6 May [Online]. Available at: http://tutor1.net/wikiquote/17148 (Accessed 14 May 2019).

Jones, R. E. (2013) *Clampdown: Pop-Cultural Wars on Class and Gender*. Zer0 Books, Hants.

Goldie (1994) *Inner City Life* [CD]. London Music Stream / Because Music, London.

The Libertines (2002) *Up the Bracket* [CD]. Rough Trade, London.

Babyshambles (2005) *Down in Albion* [CD]. Rough Trade, London.

Wolf, Patrick (2003) *Lycanthropy* [CD]. Tomlab, London.

Crook, L (2005) *Halloween*, Tap 'n' Tin, [CD]. London.

Billy Childish, Chatham Town Welcomes Desperate Men (2009) YouTube video, added by ipoems [Online]. Available at https://www.youtube.com/watch?v=Aztulcg9ipM (Accessed 12 February 2020).

Libertines, The (2002) *What A Waster* [CD]. Rough Trade, London.

Hudson Henry, The Rise and Fall of Young Sen (2015) Youtube video, added by Sotheby's [Online]. Available at https://www.youtube.com/watch?v=DoLoeQmcTo4 (Accessed 12 February 2020).

Hogarth, W. (1739) A Rake's Progress [paintings]. Sir John Sloane Museum London. Available at https://www.soane.org/collections/highlights/picture-room (Accessed 12 February 2020).

Wolf, Patrick (2005) *Wind in the Wires* [CD]. Tomlab, London.

Marquis de Sade (1997 ed.) *The Lust of the Libertines*, Velvet Publications, London.

Welsh, P. (2011) *Kids in The Riot: High and Low with The Libertines*, Omnibus Press, London.

Chapter 17 Pencil Skirts and Motorway Modernism – The Long Blondes and Black Box Recorder

Crook, L (2005) *Halloween* [CD]. Tap 'n' Tin, London.

Black Box Recorder (2000) *The Facts of Life* [CD]. One Little Indian, London.

Black Box Recorder (2003) *Passionoia* [CD]. One Little Indian, London.

Pidd, H. (2006) 'We Want Artistic Freedom'. Guardian, 3 March [Online]. Available at https://www.theguardian.com/music/2006/mar/03/popandrock (Accessed 12 February 2020).

Double Indemnity (1944) Directed by Billy Wilder [Film]. New York, Paramount Pictures.

The Long Blondes (2006) *Someone to Drive You Home* [CD]. Rough Trade, London.

Hatherley, O. (2011) Uncommon: An Essay on Pulp, Zero Books, Winchester.

No Sex Please, We're British (1973) Directed by Cliff Owen [Film]. London, Columbia Pictures.

The Long Blondes (2005) *Separated By Motorways* [CD]. Rough Trade, London.

Kate Jackson (2011) *Wonder Feeling* [CD]. The Vinyl Factory, London.

Chapter 18 Tennis Courts, Cellos and Yorkshire Valleys – Goldfrapp and My Summer of Love

My Summer Of Love (2003) Directed by Pawel Pawlikowski [Film]. London, ContentFilm.

Happy Valley. (2014). BBC One, 28 January.

Goldfrapp (2008) *Seventh Tree* [CD]. Mute Records, London.

Alison Goldfrapp and Will Gregory, Mona On the Tennis Court (2005) Youtube video, added by Lily Lacroix [Online]. Available at https://www.youtube.com/watch?v=PxOlkzmMADM (Accessed 12 February 2020).

Alison Goldfrapp and Will Gregory, Meeting in the Moors (2005) Youtube video, added by Lily Lacroix [Online]. Available at https://www.youtube.com/watch?v=Fk-IeOsj0Fw (Accessed 12 February 2020).

Chapter 19 Non-Place and Negative Space – Gazelle Twin and JG Ballard

The Cure (1989) *Disintegration* [CD]. Fiction, London.

Gazelle Twin (2011) *The Entire City* [CD]. Anti-Ghost Moonray, Brighton.

Gazelle Twin (2014) *Unflesh*, [CD]. Anti-Ghost Moonray, Brighton.

Ballard, JG (1975) *High Rise*. London: Jonathan Cape.

Ballard, JG (1962) *The Drowned World*. London: Berkeley Books.

Ballard, JG (1974) *The Concrete Island*. London: Jonathan Cape.

Mankowski, G. (2014) 'I Get Off On Intense Atmospheres: An Interview with Gazelle Twin'. Pop Matters, 22 May [Online]. Available at: https://www.popmatters.com/182045-i-get-off-on-intense-atmospheres-an-interview-with-gazelle-twin-2495657044.html?rebelltitem=1#rebelltitem1 (Accessed 12 February 2020).

Auge, M. (1995 ed.) *Non-Places, Introduction to an Anthropology Of Supermodernity*. London: Verso.

Chapter 20 Looking for Albion

Clarke, R. (2016) 'These links show Jeremy Hunt's deception over the 7-Day NHS', The Guardian, 22 August [Online]. Available at: https://www.theguardian.com/commentisfree/2016/aug/22/leaks-flaws-jeremy-hunt-deception-seven-day-nhs (Accessed 14 February 2016).

Harvey, P. (2011) *Let England Shake*, [CD]. Island, London.

Author Biography

Guy Mankowski was singer in the signed band Alba Nova. He trained as a psychologist at The Royal Hospital for Neurodisability in London. His debut novel, *The Intimates*, was chosen as a 'Must Read' title by New Writing North's Read Regional campaign. His second novel, *Letters from Yelena*, was researched in the world of Russian ballet after he was awarded an Arts Council Literature Grant. The novel was adapted for the stage and used in GCSE training material by Osiris Educational. His third novel, *How I Left the National Grid*, was written as part of his Creative Writing PhD at Northumbria University which he completed in 2015. 'An Honest Deceit' was a New Writing North Read Regional title. He is a Fellow of the HEA. He has had short stories, novellas, journalistic work and academia about music published and is a full-time lecturer in Creative Writing at Lincoln University.

CULTURE, SOCIETY & POLITICS

The modern world is at an impasse. Disasters scroll across our smartphone screens and we're invited to like, follow or upvote, but critical thinking is harder and harder to find. Rather than connecting us in common struggle and debate, the internet has sped up and deepened a long-standing process of alienation and atomization. Zer0 Books wants to work against this trend. With critical theory as our jumping off point, we aim to publish books that make our readers uncomfortable. We want to move beyond received opinions.

Zer0 Books is on the left and wants to reinvent the left. We are sick of the injustice, the suffering, and the stupidity that defines both our political and cultural world, and we aim to find a new foundation for a new struggle.

If this book has helped you to clarify an idea, solve a problem or extend your knowledge, you may want to check out our online content as well. Look for Zer0 Books: Advancing Conversations in the iTunes directory and for our Zer0 Books YouTube channel.

Popular videos include:

Žižek and the Double Blackmain

The Intellectual Dark Web is a Bad Sign

Can there be an Anti-SJW Left?

Answering Jordan Peterson on Marxism

Follow us on Facebook
at https://www.facebook.com/ZeroBooks and Twitter at https://
twitter.com/Zer0Books

Bestsellers from Zer0 Books include:

Give Them An Argument
Logic for the Left
Ben Burgis
Many serious leftists have learned to distrust talk of logic. This is
a serious mistake.
Paperback: 978-1-78904-210-8 ebook: 978-1-78904-211-5

Poor but Sexy
Culture Clashes in Europe East and West
Agata Pyzik
How the East stayed East and the West stayed West.
Paperback: 978-1-78099-394-2 ebook: 978-1-78099-395-9

An Anthropology of Nothing in Particular
Martin Demant Frederiksen
A journey into the social lives of meaninglessness.
Paperback: 978-1-78535-699-5 ebook: 978-1-78535-700-8

In the Dust of This Planet
Horror of Philosophy vol. 1
Eugene Thacker
In the first of a series of three books on the Horror of Philosophy,
In the Dust of This Planet offers the genre of horror as a way of
thinking about the unthinkable.
Paperback: 978-1-84694-676-9 ebook: 978-1-78099-010-1

The End of Oulipo?
An Attempt to Exhaust a Movement
Lauren Elkin, Veronica Esposito
Paperback: 978-1-78099-655-4 ebook: 978-1-78099-656-1

Capitalist Realism
Is There No Alternative?
Mark Fisher
An analysis of the ways in which capitalism has presented itself
as the only realistic political-economic system.
Paperback: 978-1-84694-317-1 ebook: 978-1-78099-734-6

Rebel Rebel
Chris O'Leary
David Bowie: every single song. Everything you want to know,
everything you didn't know.
Paperback: 978-1-78099-244-0 ebook: 978-1-78099-713-1

Kill All Normies
Angela Nagle
Online culture wars from 4chan and Tumblr to Trump.
Paperback: 978-1- 78535-543-1 ebook: 978-1-78535-544-8

Romeo and Juliet in Palestine
Teaching Under Occupation
Tom Sperlinger
Life in the West Bank, the nature of pedagogy and the role of a
university under occupation.
Paperback: 978-1-78279-637-4 ebook: 978-1-78279-636-7

Ghosts of My Life
Writings on Depression, Hauntology and Lost Futures
Mark Fisher
Paperback: 978-1-78099-226-6 ebook: 978-1-78279-624-4

Sweetening the Pill
or How We Got Hooked on Hormonal Birth Control
Holly Grigg-Spall
Has contraception liberated or oppressed women?
Sweetening the Pill breaks the silence on the dark side of hormonal
contraception.
Paperback: 978-1-78099-607-3 ebook: 978-1-78099-608-0

Why Are We The Good Guys?
Reclaiming your Mind from the Delusions of Propaganda
David Cromwell
A provocative challenge to the standard ideology that Western
power is a benevolent force in the world.
Paperback: 978-1-78099-365-2 ebook: 978-1-78099-366-9

The Writing on the Wall
On the Decomposition of Capitalism and its Critics
Anselm Jappe, Alastair Hemmens
A new approach to the meaning of social emancipation.
Paperback: 978-1-78535-581-3 ebook: 978-1-78535-582-0

Enjoying It
Candy Crush and Capitalism
Alfie Bown
A study of enjoyment and of the enjoyment of studying. Bown asks what enjoyment says about us and what we say about enjoyment, and why.
Paperback: 978-1-78535-155-6 ebook: 978-1-78535-156-3

Color, Facture, Art and Design
Iona Singh
This materialist definition of fine-art develops guidelines for architecture, design, cultural-studies and ultimately social change.
Paperback: 978-1-78099-629-5 ebook: 978-1-78099-630-1

Neglected or Misunderstood
The Radical Feminism of Shulamith Firestone
Victoria Margree
An interrogation of issues surrounding gender, biology, sexuality, work and technology, and the ways in which our imaginations continue to be in thrall to ideologies of maternity and the nuclear family.
Paperback: 978-1-78535-539-4 ebook: 978-1-78535-540-0

How to Dismantle the NHS in 10 Easy Steps (Second Edition)
Youssef El-Gingihy
The story of how your NHS was sold off and why you will have to buy private health insurance soon. A new expanded second edition with chapters on junior doctors' strikes and government blueprints for US-style healthcare.
Paperback: 978-1-78904-178-1 ebook: 978-1-78904-179-8

Digesting Recipes
The Art of Culinary Notation
Susannah Worth
A recipe is an instruction, the imperative tone of the expert, but
this constraint can offer its own kind of potential. A recipe need
not be a domestic trap but might instead offer escape – something
to fantasise about or aspire to.

Paperback: 978-1-78279-860-6 ebook: 978-1-78279-859-0